HOW TO HUNT

HOW TO HUNT

A basic guide to hunting big game, small game, upland birds, and waterfowl.

Dave Bowring

Winchester Press

Book design by Richard A. Kenerson

Library of Congress Cataloging in Publication Data
Bowring, Dave.
  How to hunt.
  Includes index.
  1. Hunting. I. Title.
SK33.B69   799.2   77-26746
ISBN 0-87691-251-X

Published by Winchester Press
205 East 42nd Street
New York, NY 10017

Winchester is a Trademark of Olin Corporation used by Winchester Press,
Inc., under authority and control of the Trademark Proprietor.

Printed in the United States of America.

Dedication

To the late Frank Hight, who tried to instill in me an appreciation of good bird dogs, good whiskey, and piano music.
Two out of three ain't bad.

CONTENTS

HOW TO HUNT

Chapter 1

HUNTING NUMBER ONE— THE COTTONTAIL

It is a scene repeated again and again every autumn in the country-side all across America. Several brightly clad hunters form a line, moving abreast through clumps of honeysuckle, tight weed patches, open woodlots, and brushy creekbeds. Keeping a few yards ahead are a couple of beagles, noses vacuuming the frozen weeds while a pair of white-tipped tails lash back and forth with anticipation.

The party approaches a particularly thick clump of brush and the hounds dive into it. There is a moment of silence, then the cold air is filled with the yelps and bawls of beagles ecstatic with the hot scent of fresh rabbit. The gray-brown little cottontail bounces from the far side of the cover, quickly leaving the hounds behind. The older hound, a bit slower than his companion but always the better strike dog, unwinds the scent trail, yelps out the discovery, and the two dogs line out on the new trail of hot scent. The hunters know what to do. The dogs will push the rabbit just fast enough to keep it moving, and within fifteen minutes the rabbit will close its roughly circular path and bounce within range of one of the guns. The hunters quickly look for small patches of open cover and take stands nearby. If tree stumps or a rock pile are close, each hunter may climb atop this precarious platform where his elevated position makes it easier to look for the rabbit.

About the time all the hunters are in position, the sounds of the belling hounds, until now slowly fading with distance, gradually become louder and more distinct. The rabbit has turned and is heading back. The hunters cease all movement except for straining their eyes; the rabbit can spot even small movement and turn away at the last moment. The hounds' long, musical crescendo gets louder and louder and finally the hunter farthest to the left spots a tiny bit of brown moving along the edge of the creekbed. The rabbit, so far ahead of the hounds that it merely loafs along, enters an opening in the brush. A 12-gauge shotgun is quickly thrown to shoulder and fired, the rabbit leaps in the air and falls, slipping down the frozen creekbank and kicking feebly. The smiling hunter strides quickly to the rabbit, lest the hounds arrive first and carry his prize into the weeds. "I got 'im!" he shouts, and his companions leave their posts to begin another sweep through the cover.

How many times is this and similar scenes repeated across the United States each fall? A rough estimate puts the annual harvest of cottontail rabbits above twenty-five million, making this plentiful, bouncy little mammal easily the top game animal on the continent.

Although there are over a dozen species and some seventy subspecies of cottontail rabbits, there are only six major groups in this country. The eastern, and easily most common, cottontail (*Sylvilagus floridanus*) is found from the Atlantic Coast to the Rockies. The Rocky Mountain cottontail (*S. nuttalli*) is somewhat grayer in coloration and ranges from the Great Plains into the Southwest to the Sierra Nevada. The larger, browner Audubon cottontail (*S. auduboni*) is found from Oklahoma into the Rockies and throughout the Southwest. Two groupings, found in various parts of a range from the lower Atlantic Coast, through Florida and across the Gulf States into Texas, are the small, dark marsh rabbit (*S. palustris*) and its close cousin, the swamp rabbit or cane-cutter (*S. aquaticus*). The brush rabbit (*S. bachmani*), found throughout the West, is the smallest and darkest among the six groups.

Were it not for the amazing reproductive potential of the cottontail, the species would have disappeared centuries ago. It is prey for a wide variety of predators—hawks, owls, minks, weasels, opossums, housecats, foxes, coyotes, you name it. Yet, not only has the species survived, it has spread. It has been estimated that a single pair of cottontails, with the reproductive help of their offspring, could produce 350,000 rabbits in as little as five years. Given good habitat and two acres to roam, a few rabbits left for seed following each hunting season can supply more than enough offspring to feed both wild predators and several families hungry for rabbit stew.

Habitat is the key. Good rabbit cover may vary with its geographic location, but the creature definitely prefers the edges of woodlots, cropfields, brushy fencerows, and overgrown creekbeds winding through picked fields. If the cover is thick enough to support rabbits through a hard winter, it surely contains a good supply of food as well. And if that cover just happens to be alongside a farmer's field of corn, grain, soybeans, or vegetables, the cottontail will happily add these delectables to his menu.

A few farms, because they contain all the basic requirements needed by a stable rabbit population, provide amazing amounts of quality hunting year after year. Cherrybend Pheasant Farm, covering 375 acres near

Wilmington, Ohio, is managed so as to retain as much overwintering ground cover as possible, yet full harvests of corn are produced there every fall. For the four-year period ending in January 1977, the farm's hunters collected a confirmed total of 648 cottontails during the state's rabbit season from mid-November through late January. That's an average of 162 rabbits every year. And this isn't overgunning; more than enough cottontails were left in the field both to maintain the species and provide extra for future hunting. In a few ideal situations, farms can produce up to six or eight cottontails per acre.

It's as if nature knew in advance that rabbits would be a top menu item for so many predators. A healthy adult doe rabbit can give birth to as many as three separate litters per year, each litter consisting of from four to seven offspring. And the doe, true to her task in life, often mates immediately after the birth of one litter, effectively starting the reproductive process once again before her present offspring are a day old.

As the time of birth nears, the doe may select up to half-a-dozen locations within a two-acre area, doing a bit of minor excavation at each to create a shallow nest or depression. A day or two later she chooses one site and gathers grass to line the nest, adding tufts of soft hair from her own belly, which she pulls out with her teeth. Another coverlet is created from the same materials, and once the offspring are nested and the coverlet is in place, the spot seems to fade into its surroundings, so accurate is the camouflage.

The doe spends most of her time away from the immediate nest site, either squatting in a nearby form or feeding a bit farther away. The young are nursed morning and evening, plus perhaps once during the night. Early in their young lives, the small rabbits gradually abandon the nest site, sometimes urged along by the doe, now anticipating the arrival of another litter.

Cottontails are surprisingly fragile animals. Seldom does an entire litter survive; in their sunken nest they are subject to flooding rainfall, melting snow, late frosts, and predation by marauding crows, snakes, rats, and housecats. Studies taken before and after state hunting seasons show that over 90 percent of all rabbits surviving human hunters were only one year of age. Those as old as three comprised less than 3 percent of the total population.

While the doe cottontail restricts her home territory to two acres or less (within which she will tolerate no other adult females), the male rabbit may occupy up to thirty acres. This area will include the territories of several does, and it may overlap the home of other males. The males may do gentle battle now and then, charging and hopping over one another, and perhaps giving their rivals a thumping kick with both hind feet, but such combat very rarely results in injury.

There are several excellent reasons to hunt and eat cottontails, not the least of which are their great availability. A cottontail also tastes

Ohioan Harold Barefoot admires a pair
of fat cottontails. Surrounded by baked
potatoes and carrots, wild rabbits make
tasty tablefare.

delicious in so many recipes, and its meat is far lower in cholesterol because it does not store body fat. Diseases infecting rabbits seldom are of any concern to man if care is taken when gutting and skinning the animals, and if the meat is well cooked before eating. Tularemia, or "rabbit fever," can be transferred to man but is rare enough to cause only minor concern. The insects transferring rabbit diseases hibernate in winter, while those rabbits already infected will soon die off, leaving the rest of a local population quite healthy.

Any hunter who has emptied his shotgun at a fleeing rabbit while hitting nothing but the ground and a few weeds probably believes that the cottontail flies over the ground at something approaching the speed of sound. Well, you can stop using that excuse; the cottontail's top speed won't hit the twenty mile per hour mark. More likely its surprise getaway tactics and zigzagging route caused the miss. In fact, that fluffy white flag raised by a fleeing rabbit hardly signifies surrender. Where a moment ago only weeds and fallen leaves were to be seen, now there is that intimidating white tail bouncing away, offering what appears to be an easy target. It isn't, as all of us bunny hunters can attest. Many hunters, particularly those without dogs who walk up and flush their own rabbits, shoot at the white tail, often placing their shot load behind the rabbit and missing it completely. If cover isn't too thick and you can remember this, wait a moment longer before shooting, while putting your shotgun's front bead about 18 inches in front of the rabbit's nose. Such a lead at most ranges should permit the rabbit to run headfirst into the shot pattern, killing the rabbit neatly and quickly with a headshot while leaving the remainder of the animal unpunctured by lead.

Walking up your own rabbits can be very exciting. You never know when that furry ball will squirt out, highballing it across the field for cover. There is no dog to make the rabbit circle, so you know you'll have only one or two snap shots before the animal makes good its escape. As a youngster growing up with the good fortune of several relatives owning small, brushy farms, I seldom lacked for a place to hunt, only someone to hunt with. I owned no hound, so most of my rabbit hunting was done alone, tramping through brier patches, honeysuckle tangles, and thorny stands of locust trees. If a rabbit got up in front of me, I had to train myself to shoot right then in such dense cover, before the rabbit disappeared. Seldom did I get more than one shot at a time, partly because the cover was so thick and partly because my father had the good sense to make my first shotgun a single-shot affair. It was a black-stocked H&R Topper with a two-position hammer and a full-choke barrel. With only one shot to my name, I had to make the most of every rabbit flushed. And once flushed, the rabbit was either killed outright by the tight pattern, or missed altogether. I seldom wounded a rabbit with that old 16-gauge, and in fifteen years of hard hunting the gun needed repair only once, a new sear pin. I sold it ten years ago for $15 and as far as I know it's dispatching rabbits yet.

As fondly as I recall those days, I've come to believe, however, that two can jump rabbits more efficiently than one, particularly where the cover consists of small clumps of plant tangles, brush heaps, lumber piles, and other such bunny-attractors. By putting the cover between themselves, two hunters can cover all avenues of escape. Two hunters can effectively hunt brushpiles, too. One hunter climbs atop the pile, jumping up and down to flush out any bunny that might be hidden below, while his partner stands off a few yards, ready to throw the shotgun up and fire should a rabbit flush from the pile.

Brushy fencerows, excellent rabbit cover during mild weather, suit two hunters just fine. One takes one side of the row while his buddy takes the other. Any rabbit flushing from such cover will show itself to one or the other of the hunters. Creekbeds with undercut banks and old, elevated railroad rights-of-way also lend themselves to a pair of hunters walking up rabbits. In fact, both of these places are top rabbit hotels during severe weather. The bunnies like to hide from the wind and the wet by sitting under overhanging creekbanks and in abandoned wood-chuck holes found in earthen railroad rights-of-way. Be sure to check state laws before venturing onto railway property; in some states it is prohibited, and in others prior permission is required.

If you're not alert, sometimes it can get downright hairy. A friend, my two beagles, and I were hunting an elevated right-of-way one winter morning and we foolishly let the dogs dawdle behind while we crossed a railroad bridge with rather wide gaps between the rail ties. A train thundered around a nearby curve while my dogs were no more than half-way across. Poor footing prevented them from running, and for a moment I froze, sure both animals would be crushed by the train. Just as foolishly,

Let me out, boss, and I'll find you a rabbit. These beagles have cottontails on their mind.

perhaps, I bolted back onto the bridge, scooped up two handsful of hounds, and raced back off the bridge, the train hard behind. No one was hurt, but it took my heart a good hour to drop back down to its steady seventy-two per. Now I'm a little more careful.

An uncle showed me a trick that works well for one or two hunters without dogs. It involves making use of the cottontail's bowstring-tight nerves, and nearly always results in a close, if quick, shot at the fleeing cottontail. When cover suspected of holding a sitting rabbit is too thick or thorny to be walked through, my uncle would move slowly toward the cover while scuffing his feet noisily in the ground cover. If the rabbit still hadn't flushed when the cover was reached, he would stand as close to the cover as possible while clicking one of those children's toys that is supposed to imitate the sound of a mouse or cricket. Apparently this animal-like sound, when combined with the close proximity of a hunter, snaps the rabbit's nerves and it bolts for freedom. Shots from such situations are usually of the snap variety, and more than once I've seen my uncle roll a rabbit with a shot from the hip.

Here's another tip. When you think you've put shot into a rabbit but cannot locate it following the shot, don't give up right away. Look in the vicinity of the rabbit's flight for any small opening, particularly a game or man-made trail through dense cover. For some reason, shot cottontails often seem to die at such locations, making them easy to find and reach.

If the bunny dies within sight but far inside a bush or pile out of arm's reach, break off a small green tree limb, leaving the broken end full of splinters and wooden shards. Then push the broken end of the limb into the cover and press it firmly into the loose side fur of the rabbit. Twist the stick one full revolution, then draw the animal to you as if the stick were a rope. I've used this trick many times and it sure beats getting your face and hands full of thorns.

Another method for scoring on cottontails without the aid of a hound can be employed by two, three, or four hunters in rather dense cover laced with well-defined game trails. One or two hunters choose spots where several trails converge, then look for a tree, stump, or rock on which they can perch. The other hunters move back and forth through the cover, and the rabbits they disturb move along the trails where the standers are waiting. This is very easy shooting and can be effective and fun if a .22 rifle or even a pistol is used.

I guess I've hunted rabbits just about every way there is, but I still insist the most enjoyable day afield is the one behind energetic, yapping little beagles, or maybe the slower races run by deep-howling, sadsack bassets. Hounds make the hills ring with the yapping, jump more rabbits than the lone hunter would ever see, and make losing wounded game a thing of the past. Many is the time I've hunted with my two beagles, Jay and Missy, and had them open up on a hot scent less than 10 feet from where I had just walked. The rabbit had merely left the scene without my seeing it, but there was no fooling those dogs. They'd tear off into the brush, Jay always insisting on running out in front until he missed a check, and slower, methodical Missy undoing the mistake and refusing to bark until she'd found the hot scent again.

The beagle is a bouncy, friendly little dog as ready to bring your rabbit around as it is to romp with the kids or curl up by the fire. In fact, not too many years ago, records kept by the American Kennel Club indicated the beagle was this country's most popular breed.

The rabbit hound does so much more for the hunter than just keep after that bunny until it circles back to the gun. If there is a brushpile or brier thicket around, most good hounds will crawl, wiggle, or whine their way into it, no matter how destructive the effort. And I am always amused by how fast that same dog can depart such a thorny hell when it's following a freshly laid rabbit trail. Some beagles are excellent strike dogs, and are usually the first in the pack to jump a rabbit from its form. Other, slower hounds are good at unraveling confused scent trails, while still others will not utter a sound until they smell smoking-hot rabbit scent. Each has its specialty, and the good hunter learns to recognize the personality of each hound he runs.

Whatever the characteristics of each hound, however, the man who runs it is bound to have more fun while afield and more game for the table. Friend Steve Roth and I used to hunt a ten-acre woodlot filled with thorn tangles and downed timber, and it was just the right size for one of our favorite cottontail hunts. All we'd do was put the hounds down on the edge of the woodlot, then separate, one of us on each side of the woods in a spot where we could shoot in several directions. The dogs did the rest. It didn't take long before one of them would jump a bunny, and it was easy to chart their progress in the chase by judging the sound of their voices. Sooner or later the rabbit would make the mistake of hopping past Steve's stand or mine, and the game bag got heavier. Each beagle was given a sniff to confirm that the rabbit was dead, and back they'd dive into the woodlot to find another one.

Woodlots like that one can be a steady source of great hunting. The woods were surrounded on all sides by cropfields, corn and soybeans as I recall. The cover inside the woods was very thick, often far too dense for us to push through. Add these things together and you get ideal food and cover for a large rabbit population. We usually hunted it four or five times each season, and we took an average of thirty or more rabbits a year there, yet the following fall always saw the lot resupplied with game.

I recall one frigid winter day when the snow lay half a foot deep and the dogs couldn't jump even one rabbit in the woods. Quite by accident, Steve nudged the base of a low-growing cedar tree in a spot where the branches touched the ground. Out popped a cottontail, until that moment warm, snug, and sheltered from the snow and wind. On a hunch we began looking for other small cedars, and sure enough found about six rabbits in less than two hours. Keep this in mind if late-season rabbits seem scarce. Try kicking a tree.

Not all good rabbit hounds are pedigreed. Many plain mutts have developed into first-class jump dogs, once they learn to hunt for the hunter and not for themselves. A friend had such a dog, a cocker spaniel named Brownie who was devoted to his master and dearly loved to harass cottontails. His owner would walk around the edges of a clump of cover while Brownie scooted and sniffed around inside. When a rabbit flushed, Brownie would yip, and if the game made its escape within view, there usually was rabbit on the table that night.

Farm dogs, particularly the smaller ones capable of wiggling under cutbanks and into dense weeds, can be excellent providers. I know a farmer who owns a crossbred rat terrier that loves to flush rabbits. The farmer waits until severe weather has driven cottontails into holes, then whistles up the dog for a hunt. The mutt, very alert and blessed with a good nose, burrows under anything large enough to hide a rabbit, flushing it for the gun.

Weather and its changes can have a noticeable effect on the numbers of rabbits you're likely to see, and where you'll find them. On bright, warm days, look for rabbits on hillsides with a southern exposure, particularly in spots where ground cover is present, yet light enough to permit the poorly furred rabbit to soak up the sun's warmth. The morning following a light snowfall, if the temperature isn't below 20 degrees or so, is a fine time to hunt rabbits. All tracks are fresh and concentrations of them, along with the telltale brown, pea-sized droppings left by feeding rabbits, mark where they have been within the past few hours.

In very cold, wet weather, rabbits have the ability to fast while sitting out the weather in some sheltered spot away from the wind and wet. At times like these, look for rabbits in the heaviest possible cover—large thorn patches, under brushpiles, inside farm tiles, under abandoned farm buildings, anywhere providing protection. When midwinter rains turn the rabbit's regular cover into a muddy quagmire, look for the animals to abandon their regular haunts in favor of dryer habitat. Believe it or not, in wet weather I've found rabbits smack in the middle of picked soybean fields, about the poorest vertical cover around. They snuggle down between muddy clods of dirt and you almost have to step on them to make them move.

Late-winter thaws are prime times for cottontail hunters. Rabbits that have been holed up are now out and about, often in numbers exceeding what you'd thought the area offered. Following the freeze the animals are hungry and anxious to browse on whatever green sprouts, woody stems, and waste grain they can find. This is often a rabbit hunter's bonanza.

I recall one clear December morning last year when the temperature had lifted above freezing for the first time in two weeks. A light dusting of snow had fallen the night before, and there was very little wind, a delightful day to be outdoors. A friend and I were hunting in a weedfield near his rural home, a smallish meadow totaling no more than thirty acres. Within two hours of the starting time of 9 A.M., we had our limit of four rabbits apiece and were trying to locate two coveys of quail normally found on the place. We never did find the birds, but we kept jumping rabbits until we quit at noon. By actual count we saw eighteen rabbits that morning in a field where we usually saw no more than half a dozen. A break in the weather, plus ideal habitat in that field, accounted for the bunny bonanza.

Arms used for hunting rabbits are as varied as the preferences of the people using them, but the hands-down winner is the 12-gauge shotgun loaded with low-base No. 6 shot. The twelve is undoubtedly the most commonly owned shotgun and low-base 6s have plenty of punch to reach and dispatch light-skinned cottontails. And, of course, the same scatter-

A load of chilled shot flips a flushed cottontail. On crusted snow, a fleeing rabbit can put a lot of distance between itself and the gun barrel.

gun can be used for squirrel, grouse, quail, pheasant and, in a pinch, with rifled slugs for deer as well.

Modern twelves come in every barrel choke, from wide-open skeet bores to super-tight fully choked barrels. Most commonly owned shotguns are bored for improved cylinder or modified chokes, which provide shot patterns at normal shooting ranges dense enough to handle most small-game chores. Whether jump-shooting or hunting with hounds, few cottontail hunters need to take shots longer than 30 yards or so, and most moderate chokes are dense enough at that range to do the job.

Shot much lighter than No. 6 does a poor job of finding its way through even light weed cover without losing an appreciable amount of velocity. Heavier shot too often does more damage to the game than desired, and of course the heavier the shot you use, the fewer total shot pellets are available.

Where legal, pistol shooting for cottontails, both sitting and running, can be very fast and sporting. The hunter may be able to spot a sitting rabbit before it flushes, killing it quickly and neatly with a headshot from close range, or, all safety factors being equal, banging away at a running rabbit in case that first shot misses. As long as only headshots are taken, even the heavier pistol calibers can be used, from .32 up to and including the .357 Magnum. But if you use the .357 to hunt rabbits, your ears are less sensitive to nearby explosions than mine.

I used to combine hounds and a semiautomatic .22 Remington Model 66 for a different kind of rabbit plinking. A large field I hunted had a weathered pile of fence rails in one corner. Weeds had grown up through the pile, making it a regular rabbit hotel, and several game trails winding through the field ended at the pile. It was a perfect place for an ambush. All that was needed was a pair of enthusiastic hounds turned loose in that field to start the cottontails moving. Once that happened, I climbed atop the pile, got comfortable in a sitting position, and awaited the arrival of game. Quite often the beagles were far across the field baying after one rabbit when another bunny, mildly concerned about all that hound talk, abandoned its spot in the field for the more secure hide under the pile. It would come loafing in, just hopping and occasionally stopping to sit up and peer back the way it'd come. Rabbits taken this way were always drilled just once in the head with a .22 Long Rifle solid point. The kill was clean and no meat was spoiled.

Some folks have the innate ability to see sitting rabbits when no amount of pointing will make the rest of us see anything but a tangle of twigs and undisturbed snow. I am not blessed with that awe-inspiring talent, although I have several friends who are. Steve Maslowski, an Ohio nature photographer, is one such fellow who amazes me with this ability. He can glance under a brushpile and see the telltale dark-brown spot of the rabbit's eye, and maybe just the tops of the animal's ears, which it flattens against its head while sitting.

I can count on one hand the number of times I have seen a rabbit before it flushed. The latest occurred in a low weed field while hunting with Harold Barefoot. We were moving across the field and stopped for a moment to chat. I happened to look down and there, smack between the toes of my boots, crouched a rabbit not yet spurred to flight even though it was flanked on both sides by a pair of Sears best. I whispered to Harold and pointed straight down.

"Well, shoot it," he said matter-of-factly.

"Not right here," I frowned. "I'll blow my feet off."

"Well, give it a nudge and shoot it on the jump," Harold replied. "I'll back you up. Wait a minute while I get in position." He moved a few feet to the left, shotgun raised.

I slowly raised my shotgun, never taking my eyes off the animal between my feet, which had yet to move as much as an ear.

"Ready," Harold said. "Give it a kick."

I nudged the cottontail with my toe. Nothing. Another nudge, a little harder this time. Nothing. "It won't run," I whispered. "Maybe it's too scared."

"Never saw a rabbit act like that," Harold said, frowning. "Hell, just reach down and grab it around the neck. Watch that it doesn't bite you. If it bites, drop it."

I remember thinking that last bit of advice wasn't really necessary.

Ever so slowly I bent over, extending my free hand inch by inch until the fingers suddenly snapped closed around the rabbit's neck. It still didn't move. In fact it was dead, frozen stiff as a board.

I'm still hearing about that one.

The bow and arrow is perfect for the patient hunter with a talent for spotting sitting rabbits. Most bowshots at sitting rabbits are no longer than 20 feet, some less than half that distance, so headshots are sought here as with the rifle or pistol. Cottontails are great first game for archers new to bowhunting. They are plentiful, make fairly easy targets if spotted before flushing, and are relatively easy to dispatch with a single shaft.

It is sometimes harder than you might think to hit a rabbit's head at a range of under 10 feet, even if the target is stationary. A rabbit's head measures little more than 3 inches in diameter, and often only the top edge is seen before the animal bolts from its form. Then, too, shooting at extremely close ranges after a spate of 30-yard practice takes some getting used to. Add to this the problems of shooting at a downward angle, and it's easy to understand those "impossible" misses.

Archery tackle need not be powerful or expensive to be suitable for rabbit hunting. A longbow, recurve, or compound bow with a draw weight of 30 pounds is bow enough. Arrows of any material—cedar, fiberglass, or aluminum—work just fine. Some hunters use blunt-tipped shafts, claiming headshots with this type of gear kill by shock and are quite efficient. Other hunters prefer scaled-down hunting broadheads, claiming the head's penetration pins the arrowed animal to the spot, even if death is not immediate.

If you do go with blunts, here's a tip: Have a friend who shoots a pistol save his empty brass casings. Spent shells of .32 or .38 can be made to slip over the business end of most hunting shafts, providing tough, effective hunting blunts. Of course, there is nothing wrong with hunting rabbits with the very same bow and broadheads you use for deer and other big game. Doing so keeps your arm, back, and chest muscles toned to the pull of your bow. A headshot rabbit done in by a 55-pound compound bow is killed just as cleanly as with lighter tackle.

Bob Cramer, a friend and avid bowhunter, has devised a clever way to assure himself and some friends of great rabbit hunting. They have discovered that industrial trailer parks completely enclosed by chain link fencing can provide great rabbit hunting. It seems such spots, with all the human activity, are intolerable to all the predators normally seeking rabbits—foxes, housecats, owls, and so forth. But the cottontails remain, unhampered by predators and reproducing to great numbers. Because Bob and his friends hunt with archery gear, quite often they are permitted to hunt where shotgunners are not. The group forms a single line, and with arrows nocked they move slowly across the enclosed grassland, taking shots at sitting and running animals. According to Cramer's reports, his group of innovative archers always has great shooting, and nearly always comes home with near-limits for everyone. This, of course, requires prior permission from the owner of the park; it's also a good idea to make sure hunting within city limits is permitted.

Many rabbit hunters field dress their animals immediately after the kill, when the carcass is still moist and pliable and the viscera is easiest to remove. The quickest and most efficient method is to make a single incision up the belly, from anus to breastbone. Then turn the rabbit over and one hard snap should put nearly all viscera on the ground. Be sure to place all entrails and attendant materials well above ground, perhaps in the fork of a handy sapling or bush. Hunting dogs, given the chance, will eat fresh entrails, and if the rabbit was carrying canine worm eggs in its system the disease will be communicated to the dogs that eat the entrails.

Some hunters also remove the rabbit's head before continuing to hunt, claiming it is merely extra weight and of no value. Keep this away from your dog as well.

At least one hunter I know, Steve Roth, uses a unique squeezing method to gut freshly killed cottontails. Steve holds the rabbit by its front legs, shaking it a bit to settle all viscera into the lower body cavity. Then, using both hands with the two index fingers touching one another, the animal is given a very firm, downthrusting squeeze just behind the shoulders. If this is done correctly, you'll be able to feel the ball of entrails move downward as the membrane holding them ruptures. Then follow the ball of entrails downward, making one more squeeze. If done correctly, all of the viscera located to the rear of the rabbit's diaphragm will have exited the body through the anus, needing only to be pulled free and deposited away from the dogs. The heart and lungs ahead of the diaphragm can be removed later with a knife.

This is a quick and easy way to gut a cottontail, and requires no knife work. But because no incision is made in the body cavity, body heat is retained and spoilage is a possibility. For this reason I do not use this method when the air temperature is much above 25 degrees, preferring the older, surer method of gutting a rabbit.

There are many state conservation departments willing to aid rural landowners in planting advantageous cover. Most states require a minimum of thirty acres or so, with a promise that the owner will permit some public hunting in the future. One Midwestern state, for example, not only provides the plants themselves, but visits the farmer to give advice on where and how the habitat should be planted.

A relative of mine owns 350 acres of prime farmland with perhaps a

Midwinter rabbits can make do with an amazingly wide variety of food. This fellow munches on some multiflora rose hips. (Photo courtesy Karl H. Maslowski)

dozen separate fields on it. Each field, in addition to the usual wire fence, is enclosed with a formidable hedge of thorny and impenetrable multiflora rose plants. The hedge was planted some twenty years ago by state game officials and today is taller than a man and habitat for quail, pheasant, songbirds, and cottontails. I enjoy putting a small hound or two into the natural tunnel formed by the hedge, then walking parallel to the hedge as the hound sniffs its way along underneath. It isn't long before a rabbit is jumped and the chase is on. Sooner or later the dog's persistence pays off and the rabbit leaves the hedge, and that's when the shotgun does its thing.

Farmers wishing to improve their farms as homes for wild things shouldn't be overly concerned with the way their land looks. A truly clean farm, one with no weeds along the fences, no brushpiles, no fallow meadows, is one with little or no wildlife. If trees are to be cut, pile the cuttings in a corner of a weed field, or along a fence. Permit dense weeds to thrive in parts of the farm not subject to cultivation, and maybe even designate ten acres or so as "wild," letting them grow as they will.

One small farm I hunted each fall included a fifty-acre field of soybeans. Over the summer, however, the field became so clogged with weeds and grasses that the farmer said to hell with it and left his crop in the field come fall. Needless to say, that single field provided more variety of game than any other on the place that winter. Rabbits, pheasant, quail, and mourning doves lived and fed there through early spring when it was plowed under for a new crop. Abandoning a cash crop like beans or corn is a considerable loss in the pocketbook, but, my, how the wildlife loves it!

The bottom line on cottontail rabbits, I suppose, is their great sport, excellent numbers, and fine fare on the dinner table. And given just a marginal place to live, despite all the housecats, owls, hawks, and foxes, not to mention hunters, there should always be more than enough next fall to make your hound—and your heart—sing with joy.

Chapter 2

SQUIRRELS

Daylight was still a gray promise in the eastern sky when Jack Shiverdecker and I parked his van along a rural highway near Camden, Ohio, and reached for our rifles on the backseat gunrack. Jack slipped out his side of the van and gently closed the door to muffle its sound, motioning me to do the same. We crossed a barbed-wire fence still invisible in the predawn blackness, and hurried across a weed field. I could feel my lower trouser legs dampen as my steps disturbed dew collected on each weedstalk.

We were after gray squirrels in a place Jack had hunted many times before. A large woods, covering nearly 500 acres of gently rolling countryside, had yielded many limits of squirrels to the man who was just a silhouette moving ahead of me to the woods.

Once inside the treeline, Jack pointed to a low ridge covered with huge trees—hickories by the look of them—and paced away in the opposite direction. Within a minute the sound of his footsteps faded and I moved toward the ridge. It occurred to me that I seemed to be making a lot of noise so I slowed the pace and tried to pick out a good spot for a stand. A large tree had fallen, and its slanting trunk made a handy backrest for a sitting hunter. I slid down against the trunk, brushed noisy leaves and woods duff from beneath my feet, and settled into the quiet. At first I heard nothing—my ears were still attuned to highway noises—but before long the natural sounds of a hardwoods coming awake made themselves heard.

The dew of the night before had been a heavy one; all around me drops of it were plummeting from high branches and battering the leafy ground. Somewhere off to my left a crow made a half-hearted attempt to get excited, but soon gave up and fell silent. A chipmunk, just visible in the early light, hopped warily from beneath a logpile to nose through some leaves. The little rodent scampered quickly back into its hideout when the sound of Jack's .22 rifle echoed through the woods. I smiled; Jack doesn't shoot unless he hits his target, so we probably had our first squirrel on the ground.

A few minutes later, I became aware that I was hearing something drop from the trees that didn't sound like dew. It was hard, whatever it was, and bounced off the lower branches before striking the ground. A little neck-craning let me see first one and then a small rain of nut cuttings come spiraling downward from somewhere high in a hickory to the right. I couldn't help tensing a little; cuttings meant squirrel.

The dropped cuttings stopped momentarily, followed closely by the rattle of claws on hickory bark (a light scraping that, once heard, cannot be mistaken for anything else), then nothing. Soon another stream of cuttings ticked the lower branches and I turned slightly to look for the squirrel.

There it was. The limb it was clinging to was no bigger around than my thumb and it swayed up and down as the little acrobat hung with its hind feet and fed with its front feet. I tried to find the squirrel's head in my 4X scope, found it impossible to get a steady target, and decided to wait until it relocated. I watched it finish the nut it had been working on, deftly cut another from a twig, and move to a small crotch to eat it. The scope's crosshairs met where the squirrel's head met its shoulders and I sent a .22 Long Rifle solid point on its way. The impact spun the gray out of the tree, bounced it off two branches on the way down, and plopped it loudly on the fallen leaves at the base of the hickory. I heard no rustling that would have indicated the squirrel was in anything except a dead condition.

You cottontail hunters will excuse me, but I believe squirrel hunting is America's oldest small-game favorite, simply because the rabbit requires edge and open land while the squirrel does just fine in mature timber such as the colonists and explorers found on this continent two centuries ago. Today's bushytailers may use fine-scoped rifles and smokeless ammunition, but our forefathers did just fine with Kentucky rifles and lead balls cast over stone hearths in some wilderness cabin. In fact, a favorite competition back in those days was the day-long squirrel hunt that sent shooters into the forest at dawn. Hunters delivered all the squirrels they could collect in a day's time and it wasn't unusual for the total bag of all the hunters to number into the hundreds of animals, enough to feed the entire community of settlers, trappers, and frontier scoundrels. And this was done with muzzle-loading rifles, mind you.

Today, the squirrel of the East (and this means the gray squirrel with the fox squirrel in second place) is not quite as numerous, what with the land opened up and the forests cut back into neat little parks and forests, but there remain more than enough bushytails to make a dewy morning in the hardwoods more than worth the time. In fact both species do rather well right in our backyard, some becoming so used to human attention they will accept nuts and other offerings directly from a person's fingertips.

Both the fox squirrel and the gray squirrel provide more early-season sport than any other American small game, and true sport it is. The bushytail is no rabbit that sits tight until a hunter has passed by; at the first hint of human intrusion into the area the wild squirrel is either off through the treetops or flattened against a branch far off the ground. It is this wariness that makes squirrels just tough enough to hunt. If we could stomp into a woodlot and knock off a limit of squirrels, how much fun would it be?

The successful squirrel hunter must know enough about his game and its habitat to see the need for preseason scouting. Squirrels are creatures of woods and edges, true enough, but not all woods contain squirrels and not all prime squirrel country can be hunted in the same manner. The type of habitat you'll look for, and the kind of shots you'll expect, depends on whether you are after gray or fox squirrels.

Squirrels of both types eat much the same diet—nuts, fruits, grains, a few berries, and so forth, collectively called mast. It is only logical to look for squirrels where the mast crop is heaviest. In lean years when mast is not plentiful, the hunter can often find concentrations of squirrels where food is abundant. One such spot I hunt every fall lies along a limestone stream. The water is lined with huge hickory, beech, and walnut trees that seem to bear mast even when other areas are barren. I can always depend on seeing at least half-a-dozen fox squirrels there, and have taken several limits over the years.

Generally, the range of both types of squirrels is restricted to the eastern half of the United States, and this huge region, from the Canadian border south to the Gulf, contains at least half-a-dozen races of grays, all about the same size (about 24 inches long, equally divided between body and the bushy salt-and-pepper tail).

The gray squirrel (*Sciurus carolinensis*) is often called "cat squirrel" in the South because of its series of mewing sounds not unlike those of a contented housecat. Its short-hair coat appears at a distance to be a uniform gray on back and sides, but closer inspection reveals hairs banded in gray, white, and even black. The belly and throat are colored a dull white and the tail is full and gray with black and white speckling. The animal's eye is its most visible feature besides its tail; the eyes are sharp and can see in a nearly complete circle (no wonder it's so tough to sneak up on a gray!). Although southern grays are slightly smaller than their Yankee cousins, the animal averages about a pound total weight wherever it is found.

The gray is not a lover of big timber, preferring smaller, thickly grow-

The gray squirrel is considerably smaller and lighter than the red and is more acrobatic in the treetops. Grays can often be found foraging on the forest floor early and late in the day. (Photo courtesy Karl H. Maslowski)

ing trees with plenty of adjoining branches that the squirrel uses as an aerial highway when moving to and from feeding, bedding, and escape areas. Anyone who has shot at a gray squirrel, only to miss and flush the animal into headlong flight through the trees, knows just how deftly the creature can negotiate swaying branches, crosswinds, and gravity's demands. At such times the shotgun takes precedence over the rifle.

Unlike the larger fox squirrel, the gray does not spend a great deal of time on the ground, although it will venture there occasionally to rummage for nuts or sniff around for buried food. Safety lies in the trees for the gray, and the animal is loath to yield this comfort for even a little while.

The fox squirrel (*Sciurus niger*) got its name, I suspect, because of the distinctly foxy coloration of its coat, which is a rusty red in much of its range, black with white nose-tip and tail-tip in the Deep South, and salt-and-peppery elsewhere. Size is more uniform, however, and often serves as an easy characteristic for determining a gray from a red. The weight may range from under 2 pounds to nearly 3 and the overall length is just over 24 inches. The fox squirrel's tail, although as long as that of its gray cousin, is not nearly as bushy and full; its hairs are shorter and the tail is apparently less useful as a balancing mechanism when the animal is aloft.

The fox squirrel spends a good deal of time on the ground, some even venturing down twice a day (morning and evening) for a drink if water is nearby. It is considerably less wary than the gray squirrel, often permitting a careful hunter in plain view to approach well within firearm range before moving off.

The red squirrel (*Tamiasciurus hudsonicus*), sometimes called piney- or jimmy-red, is seldom hunted because of its small size, but I have found these little rascals useful when their range overlaps that of their big cousins, the fox squirrels. Other hunters have agreed that the feisty little reds seem to hang around the large den trees favored by fox squirrels. So much so, in fact, that a few hunters I know make it a point to look for reds when hunting fox squirrels. Find one, they claim, and you've found both. I've seen indications that this may be true, but not consistently enough to make it a rule of thumb.

Both foxes and grays seem to be real suckers for hunters who use small, light watercraft on wood-lined rivers and streams. I think this vulnerability is due to the fact that no natural predator encountered by squirrels approaches from the water, and so when the creature is feeding or lazing where woods meet water, the woods get all its attention.

My favorite method of squirrel hunting is from a small, dull-painted canoe on a stream. This method is most effectively carried off by two hunters—one paddles the canoe while the other hunts from the canoe's bow. The two can switch off at intervals so the hunting is evenly distributed.

Harold Barefoot and I have worked this system down to a science. Harold owns a homemade fiberglass canoe with pared-down gunwales and without the high bow and stern. The craft is painted a nonreflecting

The fox squirrel is considered easier to hunt than the gray because it is less wary. The fox weighs up to 3 pounds and spends most of its time in trees, usually the largest in the woods. (Photo courtesy Karl H. Maslowski)

dark green and has no keel, and it moves over the water as silently as a shadow. Using a stroke that never takes the paddle blade from the water, Harold can move the canoe downstream and keep it under the overhanging branches of hardwood trees, just the right position to spot fox squirrels before they spot us.

The trick is to stay to one side or the other of the stream until a squirrel is spotted, then move within range slowly and carefully. You'd be surprised how close you can get to a feeding or loafing squirrel while afloat. In fact it is due to this range, plus the sometimes tippy nature of small canoes, that I prefer a shotgun while boating for squirrels. Even though Harold and I have hunted from his canoe a good bit and therefore seldom rock the craft violently, even slight movement makes accuracy with a .22 rifle chancy at best. I started using my improved cylinder 12-gauge on these floats, and while it was a great improvement over the rifle, Harold and I didn't really cut into the bushytail population until we began using his old full-choke shotgun. This piece carried a 30-inch barrel, allowing us to reach 'way out for those squirrels feeding high in a hickory or snoozing away a warm afternoon atop a towering sycamore. The shotgun's tight choke kept the pattern together, important when hunting small animals like squirrels, which can absorb a surprising amount of lead before giving up the ghost.

I suspect tightly choked 16- and 20-gauge shotguns would also be suitable for squirrel hunting, especially in situations when shots are not long and screening foliage is not too dense. For the most part, however, the twelve-bore is probably the best all-around choice if a scattergun is to be used.

Shells containing No. 6 shot seem to be the most popular loads for shotgunners hunting squirrels, perhaps because the same loads can be used on rabbits, quail, and other upland game as well. I've had good results using 6s and will stay with them, but there are hunters who swear 5s or even 4s do a better job of bringing down the meat.

The traditional and probably most sporting way to hunt squirrels is with the rifle, and the favorite caliber is the common and inexpensive .22 rimfire. Since rifle hunters get only one shot, or at the most two, before the game bolts, they must of necessity make that first shot count. The squirrel is a pretty small target, but decide you'll take headshots or nothing and you've created a real challenge.

A hunting friend of mine hunts grays with his single-shot .22 with a battered old 2X scope clamped (and taped) on top. There's no telling how old the rifle is, but it spits bullets with accuracy out to 50 yards or so and has accounted for a good many squirrel-and-dumpling dinners.

Rifle hunting requires more patience than the shotgunner needs, simply because a bullet through the haunch or shoulder probably won't drop the squirrel as a load of shot might. The rifleman must wait until he can put his slug into the squirrel's head, neck, or both shoulders, and that often means waiting until the animal has paused to listen or feed.

Add to this the fact that riflemen shoot at squirrels in trees, and the angle of the trajectory makes accurate shooting more difficult. Purists scoff at the use of telescopic sights on a squirrel rifle, preferring to collect their game with open iron or nothing. I've shot game both ways and prefer the use of low-magnification scopes on my rifles. The main benefit, to my way of thinking, is hitting exactly what I aim for. Leaving wounded or dead squirrels high in some tree because my bullet was off the mark is not my idea of good hunting or good sportsmanship, and my scope lets me avoid this situation. I don't take my snap shots at running squirrels through the scope, for the chances of my hitting the animal on the run makes the effort a waste of ammunition.

The equipment arguments even extend themselves to the type of .22 bullets to use on squirrels. Some men swear by Long Rifle hollow points, claiming that squirrels are too tough to be nailed with anything less. Others insist that LR solids pack plenty of wallop if the vital spot is hit. In any case, the rifle ammunition should definitely be Long Rifle, rather than Long or Short. I strive to anchor my game with a headshot, and either hollows or solids kill dead enough if I hit where I aim.

In choosing clothing to wear while hunting squirrels, start with dark, blending colors, and keep to the shadows as much as possible. Squirrels, like most animals, cannot differentiate between solid colors, but they can detect light-reflecting clothing on a sunny day. Almost any dark-colored clothing will do fine, and camouflage shirt and pants are certainly worth the small investment.

The next consideration in choosing hunting garb is the finish of the outer clothing you'll wear. Hard-finish, shiny fabrics should be avoided because they scrape noisily against branches, bark, and other obstacles in a way that no wild animal ever sounded. The older a shirt is, the better it is suited for squirrel hunting, because age softens fabrics. Worn blue-jeans are fine, and a soft-finish, dark plaid shirt does a good job of blending into the sun-and-shadow pattern of the woodland floor.

There's no reason to burn up or freeze just because the weather's extreme, either. There are camouflage-patterned overshirts of light mesh that are dandy for hot-weather hunting, and maybe the outfit you use for deer will double on squirrel during the late season. A dark-colored cap is a good idea in any season.

Some bushytail hunters outfit themselves with camouflage face masks, face paint and even gloves. I can understand how such extreme measures might be needed if the hunting is done in very open, sunny woods, or if the local squirrels have been hunted a good bit and have become especially wary. Local archery and bowhunting shops carry this type of specialized gear, or it may be ordered from several national mail-order houses that advertise in the major outdoor magazines.

Squirrel calls of two basic types are useful in certain situations. These are the hand-operated and mouth-operated calls, both of which imitate the normal feeding sounds made by a squirrel, or the chatter of a lone animal calling for its neighbors.

Squirrel calls are best used to locate squirrels, not actually call them within range of the gun, but I didn't know that when I saved up and bought my first call about twenty years ago. It was a wooden contraption that required that I tuck my tongue against the roof of my mouth while blowing into a slit in one end of the call. Done correctly, the call approximated the usual squirrel sounds, and I fully believed it would bring squirrels from hundreds of yards away if only I learned to do it right. You cannot imagine the hours I wasted sitting with my back against an oak bole, blowing that call and waiting for the game to appear. Many times I heard a squirrel answer my call with a chatter or a bark, but not once did all that calling bring a squirrel within range. I could have killed several limits if only I'd had the sense to go looking for all those squirrels that answered my call.

As with all game calling, the trick is to approximate the right sounds, then not to call too much. Sound off a time or two, then shut up and wait for a reply. Note the direction and approximate distance, and plan your stalk.

Not all squirrel calls are store-bought, of course. Some chaps do very well with homemade chalk boxes meant for wild turkeys, and one Georgian I know just scrapes a wooden stick up the side of his leather boot to make the right sound. Two coins rubbed together also do a fair job. Some old-timers can click and grunt with nothing but their mouth while getting wild squirrels to give away their positions. I tried this and almost strangled myself.

There are two effective methods of hunting squirrels—stand hunting and still-hunting. Each has its attractions and can be tailored to the particular whims of the individual.

Probably the most popular method is stand hunting, or sit hunting, to be more accurate. It involves getting into a good squirrel woods in early morning or late afternoon and finding a spot to look for bushytails. This might be a woods of mast-bearing trees, a woodline stretching between a denning woods and a fruit orchard, or an "edge" area where woodlot meets cornfield; in short, any place you've scouted enough to know that game is present, and maybe also know a little about its feeding and moving habits.

Prior scouting is important for both stand hunting and still-hunting, but it is especially important if you plan to hunt from just one spot. Being in the autumn woods at dawn is serene and enjoyable, but that doesn't mean the presence of a few squirrels wouldn't help things along. The hunter can assure himself of this by scouting the woods ahead of time, noting the squirrels' feeding areas, travel routes, and daily time schedule, and choosing his stand accordingly.

If you hunt with a rifle, with its greater range, choose a stand with a view of several squirrel trees. You might even use a light pair of binoculars and give those high limbs and branches a real eyeballing, especially in the afternoon hours when squirrels like to loaf on high limbs and let the breeze ruffle their tails. Spotting a resting squirrel isn't easy, but find just one and you'll know what to look for the next time.

Use the sun to your advantage. Sit with the sun at your back; this makes the most of your vision while making it tougher for a wary squirrel to spot you because it's looking into the sun and you're not. It's also a

A gray squirrel disappears behind a tree trunk. You can bring it back to the near side of the tree by tossing stones or twigs on the far side of the tree.

good idea to make sure you'll be comfortable. Check the ground for sticks or rocks that can feel as big as boulders after five minutes of sitting on them. Brush away noisy leaves from the immediate area.

I grew up believing you couldn't move a muscle while on stand, you couldn't blink, you couldn't even swallow. First my nose would itch, then a drop of sweat would tickle terribly as it ran down my back. About that time a pebble under my seat would grow to incredible size and threaten to rearrange my posterior if I didn't move. In those days, I got so wrapped up in not moving, despite all discomfort, that I never saw a squirrel within range. Squirrels within range were things other people saw and told me about later.

I later found out differently, of course, but stand hunting is a tough way to break a youngster in to bushytail hunting. It's much better to let him move about in the woods, taking what shots are offered and learning to pussyfoot up to a squirrel tree without defoliating the woods. This is called still-hunting; you try to keep still while doing it. Just like the deer hunter trying to see deer before they see him, the squirrel hunter moves a few feet between pauses, searching every possible tree and runway for the wiggle of a squirrel leg, the twin buds of its ears, the erratic waving of its tail plume.

This kind of stalking technique calls for stealthy movement and for this reason I favor soft-soled footwear and early hours. Soft soles let the foot feel dry twigs and noisy fallen leaves before the weight of the body is moved onto the foot, and early hours often find the forest floor damp with dew and considerably quieter than at other times. On cloudy mornings following a nocturnal shower, the woods will be well suited to the still-hunter and many squirrels have fallen shortly after a shower has passed. The rain prevents much feeding by the game, and it quiets the woods; not a bad combination.

A pair of hunters can help each other by slowly moving through a woods while keeping about 50 feet apart and abreast of each other. Any squirrel flushed by Hunter No. 1 sidles around a tree trunk to hide and exposes himself to a shot by Hunter No. 2. Such a cooperative partnership usually produces more game in the pot than even the best lone hunter could provide, and it's good companionship as well. Some of the best squirrel-hunting teams have been fathers and sons, by the way.

The term "squirrel dog" is a moniker hung on any canine with the eyes, nose, and inclination to chase and harass squirrels. In fact, if he'll chase squirrels you can do without the first two. Every good squirrel dog I've ever seen was of mixed breeding; many working squirrel dogs seem to have at least a few drops of terrier blood, perhaps because of this breed's innate alertness and keen senses.

All that's really needed is a dog that likes to chase squirrels. Some of these animals trail squirrel scent along the ground and bark when the trail winds up at a tree. Others keep their eyes and ears perked upward and bark or stare skyward when the senses tell them that such and such a tree contains a bushytail. Squirrel hunting with a dog, most popular in the South, means much less effort on the hunter's part. It also means he never hunts squirrels alone.

However you put your squirrels on the ground, make an immediate effort to get them safely in the game bag. Much has been written about staying put on stand after dropping the first squirrel in hopes another will show itself, but any number of supposedly "dead" squirrels I've left lying out in the open have somehow found the strength to crawl under a nearby log or hide in a brushpile where all the looking in the world will not find them. I have enough trouble locating truly dead squirrels when they fall on leaves and brush that closely matches the coloration of their coat. Once my game hits the ground I break cover long enough to go directly to it and put it away in the game bag. I'm sure I have frightened other squirrels in the area in doing this, but a squirrel in the hand is worth more than a squirrel that crawls away to die and be wasted because my eyes were too dim to spot it.

And if my squirrel happens to drop into water, as is often the case when I float streams in the fall, I make every effort to reach that critter immediately. I've seen accounts claiming that dead squirrels float, but this is exactly the opposite of my experience. Mine sink—but maybe I put more lead into my squirrels than the next guy . . .

Chapter 3

ANTLERED GAME

A red-jacketed hunter in northern Maine hunkers between fallen trees, pulls the peak of his cap down against the falling snow, and tries to think about the hunters just starting their drive a few hundred yards down the mountain. He glances at the .30-30 in his mittened hands and brushes melting snowflakes off the blue metal. It is ready.

The spot he has chosen is a good one because of its natural saddle in a ridge between two mountains. Deer pushed from their midday bedding areas far below, the hunters know from past hunts, will use this natural passageway to cross the ridge and drop down to deep woods on the other side. The hunter is off to the side of the saddle and hidden in good cover. A movement, then two more, down the mountain catches his eye. Three deer, their dark gray coats stark against a snow-whitened pine woods, are trotting well ahead of the drivers, right into the hunter's sights. He raises the rifle, squints along the rear leaf, over the front bead, looking for antlers.

There! The third deer, slightly behind the two does, has at least six, no eight points. The range is an easy 75 yards and the hunter is already smiling as his finger begins its squeeze on the trigger.

Many miles to the West, another hunter steps down off his horse, ties the animal on a long lead near some bunch grass, and walks over the rim of an arroyo and out of sight. Halfway down the far side of an open ridge he stops, settles against a boulder in a sitting position, and takes out a pair of binoculars from within his jacket. Pushing his hat to the back of his head, the hunter begins a slow glassing of the canyon's far wall. The glasses move almost imperceptibly as the hunter knows what he searches for is never easy to see, especially at midday.

There was no movement, no sound—only a faint glimmer of what could be sunlight reflected off a bit of antler. The hunter sits up a little straighter, his eyes burrowing into the far hillside. Finally the mule deer buck gives himself away by flicking one huge ear back and forth. The animal is bedded halfway up the far hillside, his back against a clump of brush while his eyes and ears continue to scan for intruders even as the deer naps.

The hunter, cautious now, eases the binoculars from his eyes, slides behind the boulder, and removes the lens caps from a 10-power scope atop his .270 rifle. He screws the scope's variable magnification to its lowest setting, scanning the far slope until the bedded mule deer is located. Then the scope is returned to its highest power, the range is estimated at about 220 yards, and the hunter tries to settle the scope's crosshairs on the animal's shoulders. Excited, and maybe suffering a bit of buck fever, the hunter takes a few relaxing breaths, holds the final one, and finds the sight picture he wants. At the smack of the rifle against his shoulder, the hunter can see the buck leap from his bed. Before the shot has finished echoing about the deep canyon, the hunter is already making his way to his trophy, piled up rump-first against a jumble of rocks, stone dead.

In the mountains not too many miles from that canyon, a pair of elk hunters are making their way through a steep forest of quaking aspen trees, called quakies in the West, enroute to a small park near the top of a ridge. The snow is old and piled in crusted drifts against the trunks of the trees, and everywhere there is sign of elk.

Reaching the park's opening, the hunters split. One moves a few yards to the left and settles against an aspen trunk. The other stalks through the woods to the park's far side. When both have been in place for fifteen minutes, one of them raises a whistlelike elk call to his lips and the frosty woods are full of the eerie, bugling call of a rutting bull elk. Two, three times the hunter calls, then keeps silent, listening. From the hunters' left, a reply sends involuntary chills up their backs. A bull, full of the rut and looking for a battle, has heard their call, answered, and is even now strutting through the dark quakies. Another bugle from the elk, this one closer, is accompanied by the crashing, snapping din made when the 800-pound animal swipes at trees and bushes on his way to battle. Boldly he leaves the treeline, snorting and pawing the frozen earth. The great head and 6-foot antlers, their whitened tines tipped with clods of earth and grass roots, move back and forth as the bull searches for the upstart foolish enough to sound a challenge.

The hunter nearest the bull, on his first elk hunt, is having a bit of a problem. It is one thing, he discovers, to spout bravado and confidence when soaking up the warmth of a hunting camp's fire, and quite another to hear a thoroughly angered, 800-pound animal come crashing through the aspens. It is not altogether from the morning chill that the young man's hands shake as he raises his rifle and tries to stop his crosshairs from bouncing all over the side of the mountain.

The bull, angered even more by not finding the upstart in this clearing, bangs the soil with his antlers and plows ridges through the grass with one forefoot. Twin plumes of hot breath spouting from his nostrils, the bull takes a few steps to return to the woods, but a stinging bullet from a .300 Winchester crashes into the side of his neck and he falters. A second shot, anchoring him to the spot, blasts his spine in two. Before he is all the way down a young man is just beginning to get his breathing under control 80 yards down the mountainside.

Far to the northeast, a hunter and his Cree Indian guide glide in a silent canoe along the edges of a nameless Ontario lake. It is still only dawn and mist rises from the lake surface and seems to concentrate in the dark firs and pines marching almost to water's edge.

Neither man has spoken in many minutes. The Cree employs a special paddle stroke that keeps the wooden blade in the water at all times and makes no splash. The hunter in the canoe's bow tries to overcome his desire for a smoke and keeps his eyes on the shoreline.

The canoe slowly moves around a point of land and there, less than 150 yards down the shore, a bull moose is belly-deep in the lake, the mist rising around him seeming to quiet the sounds of water dropping off his great, wide antlers. Still unaware of the canoe, the animal plunges his head and antlers into the lake, his rubbery lips searching for aquatic bulbs growing on the lake bottom.

Both men have seen the trophy and no words are needed. The Cree turns his paddle sideways to slow the canoe and the hunter turns to face the animal while raising his rifle. Suddenly a stray current of air brings the scent of men and canoe to the bull and he wheels about to face them, great antlers and ugly head dripping lakewater. Hunter and hunted stare at each other a moment, then the woods are full of sound as the powder behind a .30-06 slug goes off, followed immediately by a second aimed at the point where the bull's neck meets its muscular chest. There is a great splashing where the moose stood, then quiet. The bull is down, only the tip of one antler and the rounded side of his rib cage above water. The hunter, smiling broadly, reaches for that long-awaited cigarette while the Cree sighs and frowns a bit as he begins to move the canoe forward. The moose is lying in 5 feet of water fully 30 feet from shore; it will take half a day to drag him to dry land.

In a wide, lush pass in Alaska's Wrangell Mountains, a hunter and his guide lie belly down in a point of bushes watching a most impressive sight. For the past hour a herd of caribou, collectively appearing to be a forest of moving antlers and white rumps, has been parading past the cover, some animals less than 50 yards away. Although the men have seen at least fifty bulls, none carried the twin brow tines, called double shovels, the hunter has sworn to take.

If he could have spoken to his guide without alerting the animals, the hunter would have said he had seen at least a thousand caribou in the past hour, the main herd moving at a steady pace, a few strays pausing to nibble at low-growing grasses and lichens along the route. With even the cows bearing antlers, the hunter was hard put to keep his mind on those coveted double shovels. A few bulls had been good, some very good, but there were three more hunting days, the guide had said, and they could always look over more animals tomorrow if the client didn't see one he liked.

Slowly, the guide reached out his hand and tapped the hunter's boot-sole. Following the guide's pointed finger, the hunter saw three good bulls moving along the edge of the herd. All had good racks, but it was the third animal that caught and held the hunter's attention. Great, sweeping main antler beams, curving up and back from the animal's horselike head, were topped with wide palms edged with many separate tine points. And near the animal's head, twin brow tines swept straight forward, ending in slightly curved shovels just above the bull's flat nose. It is the trophy the hunter has waited for; it suddenly makes him forget the careful stalk, the seeping of cold groundwater through the knees in his pants, and the rancid smell of rotting berries from the bushes in which they lay.

Like the rest of the herd, the caribou has no inkling that man is about. He trots and walks behind the other two bulls, closer and closer to the hidden rifleman. When the bull is directly opposite, the hunter peers through his scope at the bull, pivots on one elbow for a lead of a few inches, and touches off the 7mm. The herd explodes with excitement and for a moment the bull is surrounded with milling animals. The hunter sits up stiffly and waits for the animals to clear.

There, both great antlers pointed toward the overcast sky, lies the bull, its white neck a sharp contrast to the brown-red of the tundra. The guide slaps his client on the back and suddenly the hunter finds he can stand up after all.

For most of us, America's antlered game animals are the most exciting, satisfying, and challenging quarry we will ever seek. From Maine to Alaska's remote mountain passes, the continent's antlered trophies provide the most varied big-game hunting outside Africa. It is to these magnificient animals that this chapter is devoted.

Whitetail: The Deer that Waves Goodbye

Two hundreds years ago most of the land between the Rocky Mountains and the coasts of what would become Virginia and New England was climax forest. Tall, mature stands of both deciduous and coniferous trees graced the land, shutting off sunlight to the forest floor and creating an openness in the woods at ground level belied by the density of the forests. And the whitetail deer was as scarce as spots of sunlight filtering through the towering canopy of leaves. Needing low-growing plants on which to feed, deer were not nearly as plentiful as they are today.

As the fringes of civilization spread westward, axes took to the woods and cleared mile after mile of forest, opening the land for corn, beans, vegetables, and oats. As the farmer fought the unending battle to keep

A simple box trap is still one of the most effective methods of capturing deer for movement elsewhere. This trap is located in Texas. (Photo courtesy U.S. Fish and Wildlife Service)

the wilderness from overtaking his fields, sunlight reached ground level and spawned what today are called edge plants—low-growing bushes, saplings, and woody weeds. America's deer herd then began to multiply, probably for the first time since the whitetail's ancestors crossed the land bridge from Asia millennia before.

As more and more lands opened to the plow, as well as to forest fires, floods, and other natural disasters, the deer increased and broadened their range and numbers. The process has continued until today. Vast expanses of land remain open, segmented here and there with woodlands and river bottoms and tangles of honeysuckle, all of it nearly ideal deer habitat. And where, 200 years ago, there were perhaps five million whitetails, today there are at least sixty-five million animals, and in some regions the number increases still.

The whitetail deer (*Odocoileus virginianus*) is one of North America's most adaptable animals and is the nation's most sought after big game. Man can shave away the woods, line the creeks with cement, build great cities of stone and steel—and still have a goodly number of deer around the edges, nibbling at tree nurseries and clipping off garden crops and leaving heart-shaped tracks in the grassy medians of our busiest interstate highways. Like the raccoon and the opossum, the whitetail needs only a modicum of food, cover, and water to live, and if that means bed-

A whitetail buck is fat and sleek at the beginning of the fall rutting season. Polished 10-point antlers and a swollen neck mark this animal as a prime trophy. (Photo courtesy Karl H. Maslowski)

ding down in a carefully tended pine plantation, or stealing midwinter mouthfuls of hay from western range cattle, well, it's all part of survival for the whitetail. It has learned to live close to man, gracing an early morning view from the back window of a suburban household while becoming apparently invisible once the deer season opens. It is entirely predictable but cannot be located when you want it. It'll come to a certain creek for water every morning of the year except that one morning when you wait for it there, rifle in hand. It feeds boldly in the open all summer, then becomes a nocturnal eater when the maple leaves change color. It is the most plentiful big-game animal in the country, yet only one in ten hunters gets his deer each fall.

The whitetail is big enough to be easily seen. Up to 40 inches high at the shoulder and weighing anywhere from 50 to 350 pounds on the hoof, the deer is colored a reddish brown, except in winter when its coat is a dull gray. Experienced hunters have spent entire days looking for deer known to exist inside a fenced mile-square area, and come away without seeing so much as a flick of a deer's tail.

The whitetail is present in nearly all of the United States except California, Nevada, and their neighboring regions. In Arizona it is known as the Coues or Arizona whitetail (*O. v. couesi*) where it lives in the Sonoran region and northern Mexico. In southernmost Florida lives the country's smallest whitetail, the Florida Keys deer (*O. v. clavium*), which weighs a maximum of 50 pounds and is about the height of a medium-size dog. The tier of northern states and southern Canadian provinces hold the forest whitetail (*O. v. borealis*). These and other subspecies are not always distinct, however, as the ranges of each often overlap and interbreeding takes place.

Wherever the deer exists, it has characteristics that permit it to survive. Deer hair, for example, is hollow. Each hair traps and warms a little air, permitting the animal to survive extremely cold temperatures; deer hair also does a good job of shedding water, a fact well-known among fly tyers. Deer feet, also called hooves, include two main toes, which form each half of the cloven hoof, plus two much smaller toes, called dew claws, which protrude from the upper rear edge of the hock. Deer in the Deep South and Florida's swamp country have developed especially large dew claws that, when the deer moves through swampy, soft terrain, provide additional walking surface to keep the animal from sinking too far into the bog.

All whitetails, bucks and does alike, have small, dark musk glands on the inside and outside surfaces of the lower rear legs. During the fall rutting period, bucks use this natural scent to trail ripe does like a hound might trail a rabbit. In fact, normally wary buck deer can become awfully single minded when trailing does ready to mate.

The whitetail uses three senses, smell, hearing, and eyesight, to find food, detect danger, locate mates, and generally get along in the wild.

A whitetail buck and his doe eye the cameraman warily. Whitetail bucks do not gather harems but pair off with individual does for a day or two.

Any hunter underestimating the animal's ability to use any or all of these will likely go home empty handed.

The animal's nose is perhaps its most finely tuned defense. Under the right conditions, a deer downwind from a man can detect his presence up to a third of a mile away. Because the animal breathes through its nose, it is continually testing the air for strange scents.

The whitetail's hearing is not only quite good, it's educated as well. It's been said that a wary old buck hears everything that goes on in the woods, but more important, the deer's experience tells it which sounds are natural—the passing of another creature, wind in the trees,

The art of rattling up a buck entails banging and scraping two old deer antlers together and against nearby brush to simulate the sounds of two bucks in combat. Other deer hearing this are drawn to the site.

Two prime bucks lie dead after locking antlers and starving to death. Shoving matches between mature bucks are common, but seldom do they result in this tragedy. (Photo courtesy Karl H. Maslowski)

the sound of falling dew on dry leaves—and which sounds are alien. Hunters knowing this can match the sounds they make in the woods to those that the deer finds familiar and thereby get closer to their quarry.

Some experts say a deer's eyesight isn't as sharp as its nose or ears. This may be true, but move so much as the hair on your arm when a buck is watching you 100 yards off and he'll fade into the woods like morning mist under a hot sun.

I remember one curious eight-pointer that discovered me about the same time I spotted him. We were separated by several dozen smallish white pine trees and I knew there was no way I could get a clear shot, so I decided to play a game with him. I remained hidden behind a tree trunk for a few seconds, then leaned to the left to reveal my head and shoulders. The buck leaned the same direction, staring at me intently. I slowly disappeared behind my tree again, waited a few seconds, then leaned to the right. Out popped the deer's antlered head again, staring in wonder at this nutty human who wouldn't stay put. We kept at it for another minute or so, then the buck tired of the game, snorted, and bounced off through the pines, his white tail and rump patch waving goodbye until lost among the trees.

A relatively small number of hunters prefer to use primitive weapons for deer. Young Steve Woods killed this massive whitetail in Ohio with a .58-caliber muzzle-loading rifle.

The deer's snort, which sounds like a sharp blowing of air through its nostrils, can be used to clear an unpleasant scent from its nose as well as to register nervousness and to alert other deer. But it can also be used to frighten the hell out of a deer hunter.

There are four basic methods used to hunt whitetails, although local customs and conditions often cause hunters to alter and combine them for better results. They are the deer drive, still-hunting, standing, and the use of specially bred and trained deer hounds, with the latter method most popular in the Deep South.

The drive does just what the name implies—moves deer in a predetermined direction past waiting hunters. The method is effective in country with natural land features that may be made use of to help channel the drive, such as ravines, tall ridges, known deer bedding areas, and wide creekbeds that deer might use as travel routes when fleeing. From five or six hunters on up to a dozen or more can participate in a deer drive. Usually, at least one of the party is familiar with the sur-

When deep snows fill the woods in late winter, hunters on snowshoes can move around much more easily than deer, especially if the snow is soft. (Photo courtesy Michigan Tourist Council)

This hefty Ohio buck fell to a single rifled shotgun slug while the deer ran from the hunter up a steep slope.

*Waiting on a deer stand is never easy,
but this deer hunter seems to be making
the best of it.*

rounding country; he knows where deer are likely to be located, which way they will move, and where the drivers and standers may best be placed. Known as the drive captain or boss, it is his responsibility to set up the drive and look after the safety of the hunters. A good captain will make sure all hunters get an equal amount of time doing the jobs of driving and standing. All that's needed on a deer drive is a slow, even movement of the line of drivers toward the suspected deer positions; this subtle pressure will move all the deer in the area at a pace slow enough to give the standers shots at animals not thoroughly spooked.

Still-hunting is the somewhat misleading term used to describe a very slow, measured movement through the woods by a lone hunter, or two hunters spaced well apart. I believe it to be the toughest deer-hunting method of all because it requires the fullest use of every sense available to man—hearing, eyesight, stalking ability, attention to natural elements such as wind direction, plus a smattering of just plain common sense, the proper interpretation of things seen and heard.

The secret of successful still-hunting is moving slowly enough, and pausing often enough, to make sure you know as much as possible about what is going on in the vicinity. Experienced hunters who still-hunt a lot learn to look for parts of deer, instead of the entire animal. Perhaps the few square inches of gray color you see through the leaves is part of a deer's ear, or maybe the odd-looking tree trunk 50 yards away is really a deer facing directly away from you.

Sometimes a hunter can take advantage of a deer's inattention as I did on a NASA federal installation permit hunt a couple of years back. I was moving very slowly along the edge of a large thicket when I happened to spot an odd shape among some trees 100 yards away. I stared at it and suddenly the animal outlines showed it to be a very good buck facing directly away from me. He paid no attention to his backtrail but seemed very intent on something in front of him. I bent over and, moving slowly across a field with cover no higher than my knees, managed to get within 50 yards of him before I feared any more progress might reveal my presence. It was then an easy matter to ease into a sitting position, flick off the safety on my slug-loaded shotgun, and put two rounds into his boiler room. Although I was completely out in the open, he had no idea I was there—and this on a closed installation where deer are hunted intensively every Saturday for several months.

Most successful still-hunters may require thirty minutes to cover 50 yards of woods, even more when the cover is dense. The method can be especially effective when a light, misting rain is falling, because deer seem to lose some of their natural wariness in damp weather. Try moving slowly through heavy bedding cover at such times, such as honeysuckle thickets, pine plantations, scrub oak, and the like. You can sometimes find a heavy-beamed old buck in his bed during light rainfall because moisture deadens the sound of your footsteps.

Stand hunting very often means just that—standing in one spot in hopes the deer will come to you. This requires a thorough knowledge of how deer move in the immediate area, an awareness of the wind direction, and the assurance that enough other hunters are in the woods to cause the deer to become restless and move from one location to another.

Stands at ground level are at their best when the hunter chooses a natural elevation, such as the edge of a cliff, the sidehill of a ridge, or a rock outcropping somewhat above surrounding terrain.

Tree stands—natural or artificial platforms nailed or lashed to limbs

Perching on a tree limb hardly gives a firm shooting platform. Tree hunters should plan ahead and use either firmly attached platforms or any one of several commercial stands on the market.

in a tree offering good observation of nearby deer trails, scrapes, or other sign—are used in many established deer states, and have just recently been legalized in Michigan, long one of the country's top producers of deer.

The best way to use the tree stand is to locate it where the hunter is most likely to see deer. This can mean any one of a number of places, such as just downwind from established deer trails, fresh buck rubs and scrapes, known bedding or watering areas, or along routes used by deer when fleeing from hunting pressure.

Jim Kunde and Bob Cramer, hunting buddies of mine, and I did a full day's scouting in southeastern Ohio recently, and along one mile-long ridge we found all the deer sign a hunter could hope for. The ridge, gently sloping downward through an open hardwood forest, apparently was the courting ground for a number of antlered bucks, judging by the profusion of buck sign we found. Seven scrapes—yard-square plots of barren earth rutted with deer tracks and antler marks and scented with buck urine—were dotted along the ridge, every one located directly

Tree stands often reflect the hunter's attention to detail. Makeshift stands needn't be fancy, but they should be located near game trails and offer clear avenues from stand to trail. The best stands are at least 12 feet above the ground. This archer has installed a makeshift seat for added comfort.

under some sort of overhanging tree branch or limb. Off to the side we found several small saplings completely wrecked by amorous bucks— bark had been horned badly and hung in strips, small branches were broken, and the earth around the saplings showed the large, wide tracks of a good buck. And to top it off, we found several narrow doe trails crossing the spine of the ridge where deer passed from one valley to another. We also saw two does jump from their beds on the day we scouted.

Jim decided on a tall, strong tree for his stand location. It was slightly uphill from the main ridge trail, and located upwind from where he ex- pected the deer to appear. Small, tangling branches were lobbed off with an axe, and a sturdy platform of planks was built in a fork about 20 feet above ground. Once in place on the stand, Jim directed Bob and me in an effort to clear out all ground-level brush that might interfere with a clear shot. All brush cut during the job was carefully bundled up and moved at least 100 yards away and off the main ridgetop, lest its appear- ance alert the deer to something out of the ordinary. Jim pronounced the stand ready and we moved on to a spot Bob had found.

The ridge's largest and freshest scrape was located smack under the leafy branches of an old hardwood. The deer would have had to nearly touch the tree trunk with his flank to make the scrape, and in that tree Bob built his stand. Two large spikes were driven into the tree for steps, and the width of the tree itself at the first fork was platform enough.

Choosing fresh buck sign to help locate stands often pays off because, once a buck establishes his route along several fresh scrapes, he'll continue to visit and freshen them with new urine at least once a day. The secret is being there when the deer is.

One final note on tree stands. Make them large enough so you can pivot around a bit in case the deer comes in from the rear, and make them stable enough so, once in the tree, you don't have to worry about toppling out backwards because a nail gives out.

Bob Cramer was bowhunting from a tree several years ago. He leaned too far backwards and fell out, landing on his back in a dry creekbed. He was knocked unconscious by the impact and had several broken ribs. After regaining consciousness, he had to crawl for over a mile until an- other hunter heard his call for help and carried him out of the woods and to a hospital. Be careful in that tree.

Muleys: Beautiful but Dumb

To the hunter used to eastern whitetails, the western deer with the ridiculously long ears must seem stupid indeed. It beds right out in the open, will often let a hunter stalk far closer than its eastern cousin, and has the rather brainless habit of bouncing away from a hunter after a close miss, only to stop broadside atop the nearest ridge to see what

There are several commercial tree stands available and all offer the hunter a steady shooting platform and mobility about its height and location.

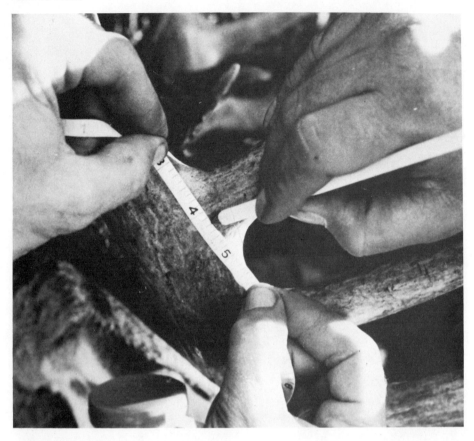

Antlers of possible record proportions should be carefully measured sixty days after the animal was killed.

all the commotion was about. More than one four-pointer has met its master during that final look.

There are three subspecies of mule deer in North America. *Odocoileus hemionus* is the animal commonly found in most of the western states. It averages 200 pounds on the hoof and, except for its ears (up to a foot long) and different antler formation, might well be mistaken for a whitetail in body conformation. The range of this animal is impressive in the variety of terrain and altitude within it. The Rocky Mountain muley is found as far west as the Sierra and the Cascade mountains, and as far east as the Dakotas, Oklahoma, and even western Missouri. The northern extreme is about the sixtieth parallel, stretching south all the way into Arizona and New Mexico.

A second subspecies is found along the Pacific Coast. The Sitka blacktail (*O. h. sitkensis*) ranges from the southeastern corner of Alaska into northern British Columbia. A third subspecies, the Columbian black-

A desert mule deer with average antlers. Racks on these animals often reach much greater proportions. (Photo courtesy Colorado Game Division)

tail (*O. h. columbianus*), ranges from British Columbia southward into the northern half of California.

Unlike the average whitetail rack, mule deer bucks develop headgear enough to impress many an eastern hunter trying muleys for the first time. A muley's rack may appear basketlike in that it is usually as high as it is wide. The average point arrangement is four points to the side, if brow tines are missing or are under the 1-inch minimum length for scoring. Also unlike the whitetail's antlers, muley racks consist of a main beam and one secondary tine on each side. Both the main beam and the secondary tine usually develop one fork apiece, thus the normal four-points-per-side count. Brow tines may or may not be present on a typically antlered mule deer. Nontypical antlers, on which a veritable forest of oddly shaped and sized points may occur, are sometimes seen and are apparently the result of a genetic alteration. Some hunters prize such

Mule deer, like elk, are forced to move to lower ranges as winter snows clog the high mountain country. (Photo courtesy Colorado Game Division)

oddities while others consider them ugly and make all efforts to avoid shooting such an animal.

And some hunters will do anything for a set of antlers, legal or otherwise. One November I was in a party of elk hunters returning to Denver by car when we passed a long shale slide south of that city. The driver, a state conservation officer and elk guide, slammed on the brakes, parked the car along the road, and headed across the highway. There, halfway up the slide, lay the carcass of a very large muley buck, a single bullet hole above the right shoulder. The deer would obviously have

An Alaskan timber wolf in his winter coat. Alaskan wolves have been the center of an argument between state officials wanting to reduce their numbers, and Lower 48 conservationists who want the wolves left alone. The battle still rages.

weighed well over 200 pounds, and all that was missing was its scalp and the attached antlers. The officer guessed that a disgruntled elk hunter returning to Denver had spotted the deer early that morning, stopped his car on the lonely interstate, and shot the animal, stopping only long enough to saw its antlers off before speeding away. The entire body of the deer was left to rot. Admiration for antlers should hardly take a hunter this far from his senses, nor so far from the truth when he invites friends to his home to brag about the big muley rack on a den wall.

In the West, where moisture is not always plentiful, muley bucks must eat what they can where they can. For this reason, muleys eat a surprising variety of plants and their products. Blacktails of the misty ranges and rain forests make a diet of bromegrass, oak, fescue, ferns, berries,

The cougar, also called puma or mountain lion, can be a natural control on mule deer numbers.

and acorns, while northern deer eat evergreens and whatever berries may be available. Desert mule deer eat what succulent plants the arid region offers, often depending entirely upon plant-stored water for their moisture needs.

As the fall mating season approaches, muleys, unlike whitetails, may band together in bachelor herds of from three up to as many as fifteen or twenty bucks. The hunter fortunate enough to happen on such a forest of racks should thank the gods—*after* he has made good his shot, however.

When the rut deepens, the muley buck may gather as many as five or six willing does in a loosely knit herd. It would be highly unusual if a whitetail buck did the same because the eastern deer usually prefers to court just one female at a time. The muley's lady friends could hardly be considered a true harem, such as a bull elk might assemble, because the does are free to come and go as they will, perhaps wandering off to join another entourage of does that are attending the wanderings of a bigger buck.

Mule deer are subject to natural predation far more than are eastern whitetails merely because they live in a region where large predators exist. Animals taking their share of muleys, especially the very young, the old, and the diseased, include the coyote, bobcat, cougar, black bear, and, in the southern Canadian provinces, the timber wolf. I have seen a pair of wolves chase a luckless deer onto the slippery surface of a frozen lake. The wolves' paws had little trouble on the frozen surface, but the hard hooves of the deer caused it to fall repeatedly while trying to flee. The big predators had no problem chasing down the deer and killing it quickly. One wolf fed briefly before moving back into the woods while its companion gorged for thirty minutes on the venison. I assumed the wolves would wait nearby and return a day or so later to finish devouring their kill.

A favorite hunting method for high range and mountain muleys is best employed by two or three hunters afoot. One hunter stalks slowly through the bottom of a draw or canyon while his companions parallel his route, one on each sidehill of the canyon. The idea is to push whatever deer the canyon holds into the path of at least one of the hunters. Muleys hunted in this manner sometimes offer only running shots, and flat-shooting calibers and tight optics are needed to do the job.

A "running" mule deer doesn't really run, at least not the way a horse or a whitetail does. It bounces along, or hops, on stiff legs. One of nature's most distinct sounds is the *whoosh* made by a bouncing muley as it lands and forces the air out of its lungs.

Glassing exposed hillsides for bedded deer, as was described at the beginning of this chapter, is a popular and productive way to hunt muleys where terrain and cover permit, especially in the high prairie of the Dakotas where rolling grasslands and wheatfield ranches drop suddenly along large streams and rivers. Such broken country provides good cover for deer and is usually easier to hunt than the high mountains.

Rifles used for mule deer tend toward lighter, faster calibers because of the considerable distance between hunter and deer. Probably the heaviest practical caliber, barring those hunts when muleys are hunted in conjunction with elk, would be the .30-06, followed closely by the .280, .270, .264, .243, and, in some cases, even the hot but light .22-250. What's needed is a bullet that will travel up to 250 yards while retaining a killing punch and without dropping excessively at those ranges. Put a slug of reasonable size through the lungs, heart, liver, or spine of even the toughest muley, and it's as good as hanging in camp. Shoot badly with a .457, and all the velocity and wallop in the world won't put the deer on the ground.

Elk–The Magnificent Deer

The American elk once ranged from its present home in the high country of the West across the northern tier of states and southern Canadian provinces into the upper Midwest and New England. As civil-

Modern, scoped shotguns are deadly for deer in states permitting no rifle hunting. Note the carrying sling.

ization pushed westward, however, the man-wary *wapiti* was forced first onto the high plains, where photo evidence indicates they were hunted to supply camp meat as well as for sport. As the pressure increased, elk moved into the mountains and foothills of the Rockies, High Sierras, and Cascades where they are found today.

To the hunter from the lowlands of the South, Midwest, or Far West, the elk would be a trophy even without its huge size (up to 1,000 pounds for a really big bull) and magnificent antlers. This member of the deer family today lives in some of this continent's tallest country, ranging from as low as 6,000 feet in some deep mountain valleys and low foothills, to midsummer ranges topping 13,000 feet where cool winds provide comfort and keep insect pests to a minimum. The mountain country itself can be more than enough challenge. Lungs used to the dense, plentiful air of sea level suddenly are asked to make do with less oxygen, and the climbing and other exercise needed daily in elk country make even greater demands on heart, lungs, and city-softened muscles.

Ross Utt, an Air Force lieutenant colonel and partner in the Colorado High Guide Service out of Denver, says his practice is to send every prospective customer a medical questionnaire. The reason, he says, is to discover the hunter's overall health condition before making recom-

Elk country is some of the world's prettiest terrain. Its extreme altitude requires that visiting hunters be in the best possible health, however.

mendations about getting in shape well before the season opens. "If a hunter can jog a mile without becoming overly tired, he's in good enough shape to hunt elk," insists Utt. Utt's elk hunts take place in the lovely and remote Flattops Wilderness Area north of Eagle, Colorado, where altitudes can reach 11,500 feet above sea level. At such heights air is thin and breathing comes hard to the man unprepared.

But for the hunter able to take the strain, elk hunting is a wonderful reason to leave city smog, noise, and lights behind for a time. Among the golden aspen leaves, green-black forests of pine and spruce, along shimmering mountain brooks alive with cutthroat trout, even an eleven-month resident of Metropolis can feel his guts unwinding for the first time in years. To stroll under a black mountain sky peppered with stars, to suck the chilly air of a Colorado night into the lungs and feel the chest swell under a double layer of woolen shirts is heady stuff.

Nights are short in an elk camp. You are no sooner asleep than an

A cow elk sports no antlers but, where cow hunting is permitted, provides probably the best table meat available.

The National Elk Refuge at Jackson, Wyoming, provides artificial feeding for great numbers of these animals when the high country is deep in snow. (Photo courtesy U.S. Fish and Wildlife Service)

ungentle hand pushes your shoulder and announces that coffee is hot and it's time to roll out. You fight your bleary-eyed way into a pair of pants, pull on a jacket, and stumble outside the tent. The camp is a fog of morning mist and blue camp smoke. Someone shoves a tin of coffee in your hand and you gulp it, choking a bit on the searing black liquid. Over breakfast you devour three eggs while watching a wrangler round up the saddle stock, remove their hobbles, and lead them to morning water. Soon it's time to check saddles and scabbards, shove a sack lunch into saddlebags, and wait for the guides to give the word to move out. The horses stand quietly now, grain-fed and apparently willing, their breath showing white plumes in the chill. Then everyone is mounted, five hunters and two guides, and the horses move single file up from camp on a path only the horses see and you think that maybe today is *the* day.

The most commonly hunted elk is the Rocky Mountain elk (*Cervus canadensis nelsoni*), which ranges from British Columbia, Alberta, and Saskatchewan down through the Rockies. Largest of the elk tribe, found in the Cascades and Olympic mountains, is the Roosevelt elk (*C. c. roosevelti),* which is in lesser numbers than those found in the Rockies. This subspecies, which may reach 1,200 pounds on the hoof, is found in the coastal forests from Vancouver south through Washington, Oregon, and northern California.

A somewhat smaller elk, found in the lower portions of Canada's prairie provinces, is the Manitoba elk (*C. c. manitobensis*). This animal

This is caribou country in northern Manitoba. Woodland caribou found here may be hunted by Manitoba residents only.

has smaller antlers than the much more plentiful Rocky Mountain elk and, in keeping with its forest habitat, is darker in color. A protected subspecies, the tule elk (*C. nannodes*) exists in small protected herds in central California and is smaller and much more pale than any other of the subspecies. Some claim the tule elk is a separate species altogether.

The National Elk Refuge, located at Jackson Hole, Wyoming, nestles within the Teton Mountains and hosts some 30 percent of the region's wild elk which are fed hay and alfalfa pellets through the Teton's killing winters. Another 50 percent of the elk are fed on special feeding areas scattered throughout the area. The rest of the region's herds refuse to depend on man for their livelihood, preferring to remain in protected river basins and thick forests, gleaning what nourishment they can from beneath several feet of powder snow.

When winter breaks here, so does the concentration of elk. Where only days before man could approach amazingly close to the protected animals, now the elk return to their wild ways and scatter into the high country, the bulls slinking off to live their summer in bachelor herds or alone, the cows now fat with calves. If next winter is harsh and the snow in the Tetons is deep, the refuge's 23,000 acres will once again see wild creatures depend on man for winter rations.

At least 90 percent of this country's annual elk harvest takes place in just six states—Colorado, Idaho, Montana, Oregon, Washington, and Wyoming, with the four Rocky Mountain states showing an overall average kill of about 15,000 animals (including both sexes), and the two states of the Pacific Northwest with harvests averaging about 10,000 elk per autumn.

There are residual elk numbers in other areas, including Arizona, New Mexico, Canada's far western provinces, Alaska, Manitoba, and even a few in North Dakota and Michigan. Wherever you hunt the elk you can bet the country will be high, wide, and breathtaking. Unless you have hunted the area before, it is likely you wouldn't have the slightest idea about where to find elk or even how to look, and the answer is a professional guide who knows the country, keeps tabs on the movements of elk herds, and knows how to field dress, quarter, and pack out a gutted elk that may weigh upwards of 700 pounds dressed.

The guide, who often doubles as an outfitter for everything from a simple drop camp to a fully equipped base camp consisting of a dozen tents, 25 horses, and a staff of cooks, wranglers, guides, and packers, can often mean the difference between seeing game and not seeing game. It is his job to know the country fully, to advise the customer on what personal gear to bring along, and to state in writing before any agreement is signed precisely what services he will provide, the total payment he expects, when it is to be made, and, just as important, a list of names and addresses of past customers with whom references can be checked before hard cash is forked over.

And do take the trouble to check his references. Hunts should be planned at least eight, sometimes ten months in advance, plenty of time to query six or eight names on the list of references to ask about camp accommodations, amount of game seen on past hunts, quality of provided food and equipment, and the hunters' overall impressions of the service. Most hunters are willing to give their opinion of past hunts if you will only ask. By all means do it.

Professional elk guides can be located through several sources. A letter requesting a list of licensed guides can be sent to the game and fish department of the state you intend to hunt. You can drop a note to the outdoor editor of the largest newspaper in the state to be hunted, and send letters of inquiry to elk guides listed in the classified section of most major outdoor magazines. If a guide writes back claiming that his hunters enjoyed an 80 percent success ratio the year before, you had better beware. Such astronomical hunter success usually means one of two things: this chap ties elk to trees for his hunter to shoot, or he only took one amazingly lucky party of hunters out the year before. Fewer than 50 percent of hunters afield after elk ever put meat on the ground, and that figure can be cut in half more often than increased.

It is extremely important to know exactly what the outfitter will and will not provide during the hunt. You'd be surprised how many hunters show up in an elk camp and, come sundown, discover they themselves, and not the outfitter, were supposed to provide sleeping bags. Rolling up in a saddle blanket with your head on a pack saddle may sound romantic, but it isn't a very comfortable way to spend the night.

And the guide, like a traveling salesman, had better know his territory.

If he doesn't, you'll have a week of the blind leading the blind. I once spent a totally fruitless week in Colorado's San Juan Mountains, not far from the New Mexico border. The outfitter-guide, who came on the recommendation of the Colorado game office in Denver, claimed to have hunted the area for years but in fact had no idea how to get around from one spot to another. We spent an entire day trying to crawl up a towering mountainside while leading horses, only to turn around and come back down again, a four-hour trip one way, when the guide announced that he didn't know how to reach the top of the mountain after all. He was also perplexed as to where the elk were at any particular moment. That was a long week, and needless to say I'll never spend good money on the likes of him again.

Once properly guided and outfitted, however, you still must locate game, and there are several ways to go about it. If your guide has done his homework, he should already know where local elk are hanging out, and may have already spotted a herd bull with your name on it. In this case he should be able to put you within sight of the animal where the terrain can be glassed and a stalk planned and carried out.

When the fall rutting season descends on elk country, mature bulls engage in shoving matches. Rarely is an animal injured in such battles, however.

Another popular method is to be situated on a raised bit of landscape at first light, seated, and with a pair of good binoculars in hand. Some of the valleys of the West can cover many miles and it is possible that you might spot a small herd of elk feeding, bedded at midday, moving to or from water, or just lazing away the day in some jackpine thicket. Early in the season, elk move from one part of their range to another, following the mating urge or the availability of food. An experienced elk guide should know the routes migrating elk use, and it's his business to put you near one or more trails or elk wallows.

If you are a bowhunter, or the state's rifle season for elk coincides with the species' annual rut, you may be able to call up your bull. This is the most exciting way to hunt these magnificent animals. Bull elk call, or bugle, to attract cows to their harems and to challenge other bulls in the area to either put up or shut up. It is an invitation to fight, a cry of frustration and anger, a pure, wild song of the mountains, and once heard it is unforgettable.

The bugle of a bull elk is a cross between a grunting groan and a whistle. It starts on a low, throaty note, well down in the chest, and quickly moves up into a falsetto that sounds ridiculous coming from an animal that weighs at least 700 pounds and is very, very angry. Bull elk can bugle at any time of day, but morning and evening seem to be preferred times. The unknowing hunter often makes the mistake of bugling too much and too often. The best bet is to bugle once or twice, wait ten or fifteen minutes for a reply, then try again. If your bull is within earshot and the call was correctly done, he'll answer soon enough.

The exciting part about bugling is, once old mossy horns answers, he is probably on his way toward you. He may come crashing his way through the woods, smashing saplings under his chest and uprooting bushes, or he may sneak to the downwind side to size up his opponent before coming into view. Or he just might come blazing out of cover and take some healthy swipes at your saddle horse, thinking it is the bull that's been throwing insults all over the mountain. Calling elk is great sport, but it can be hard on the nerves.

Most guides know how to bugle, and many of them design their own calls. It's best to let the most experienced man do the calling; you'll have your hands full soon enough.

Rifles used for elk must do two things above all else: They must be able to deliver a hard-hitting, penetrating bullet through layers of fat and muscle, and often through heavy bone, and they must be able to deliver it over considerable distances. In fact a good elk rifle is really just a souped-up weapon used for mule deer.

Although some elk have been killed at ranges under 20 feet in dense cover, most good heads are taken at ranges starting at 100 yards and sometimes approaching 250 to 300 yards. Shots are seldom level—you will often be shooting uphill or down—and the target may be moving. The secret is not to be surprised; know the elk are there and get into a solid shooting position before the moment comes.

Elk have been knocked off with about everything from a .264 up to and including the cannonlike .338. One compadre of mine will use nothing except his pet Winchester Model 70 in .270, and has seven elk to his credit. The standby .30-06 is still very popular, as is the .300 Winchester Magnum. The secret in shooting elk, as with any big-game animal, is to hit it hard in the boiler room or its immediate vicinity. Hit the lungs, liver, or heart and the animal is dead on its feet. Miss by an inch or two, and you break a shoulder. Lightly wound or miss the elk altogether, and it'll run 10 miles before slowing down. The choice is yours.

The elk can measure 5 feet at the withers and stretch 9 feet long. His antlers often tower 6 feet high and can weigh 50 pounds. He lives in this continent's most remote country and is the world's largest round-antlered deer. Some consider him the ultimate trophy, the quintessence of the hunter's life. You will have to seek him in the high country to discover why.

Moose

The first moose I ever saw won hands down. I had been fishing a small trout lake about a mile back in the bush from Lake Athapapuskow, in northern Manitoba. The trip required a short portage of about half a mile through dense lakeside pines and hardwoods on a path deeply rutted and carved through the trees by generations of moose.

The rainbow trout in that lake had a habit of feeding on surface insects from late dusk until well after dark, and the dry-fly action we enjoyed had kept us on the water until only a faint red glow in the west showed where the sun had been; all else was pitch black.

With no flashlight, a flyrod in one hand and a fine catch of trout in the other, I led the way along the hard-packed path through the woods to a waiting boat on the big lake. Navigation in such blackness was accomplished by aiming our steps in the direction of the oval of slightly lighter blackness along the path. I was in front, trying to keep my rod tip out of trees, when the opening in the bush suddenly disappeared. It just wasn't there anymore.

"I must have lost the path," I said to the Cree guide. "We must be in the trees."

"Moose," he said in a rather reverent tone of voice. "She is close. Stand still."

Then it dawned on me. The path had vanished because we had met a moose coming the other way. Her bulk had so filled the path that it shut out the bit of remaining light. Then I smelled her. It was a heavy, musky odor, suddenly very strong, the kind of smell only a nearby animal could emit.

A full minute of silence followed. Then the huge animal tossed her head and snorted. I swear I felt her hot breath. Then the guide grabbed my arm and shoved me off the path and into the trees. I fell, dropped the rod and fish, and went flat on my face. "She come," the guide explained from a prone position beside me. Then the sound of a heavy animal trotting past us slowly faded as the moose made her way off into the bush.

Although temporarily shaken, the incident had no real lasting effects. After returning to the lodge, gulping a couple of stiff drinks, and having a change of shorts, I was fine. I never got a good look at that animal, but

A pair of Alaskan bull moose, the world's largest members of the deer family, make a valley ring with the crash of their heavy antlers. Such fights are common during the fall rut. (Photo courtesy Alaska Department of Fish and Game)

afterwards it was easy to understand how this great northern member of the deer family got to be the target of so many erroneous beliefs, legends, and just plain untruths.

It is easy to understand how tales of this great forest deer got started. Moose, wherever they are found, are immense beasts, standing from 6 feet at the withers in Wyoming to well over 7 feet in prime areas of Alaska. Moose are large, sometimes weigh as much as 1,800 pounds, and can, on real trophy bulls, sport antlers over 70 inches wide and weighing nearly 90 pounds.

There are seven subspecies of moose, including four in North America, two in Asia, and one in Europe. On this continent the moose population is broken into three geographic distinctions. The smallest of America's moose live in and around Wyoming and number about 3,500 animals. *Alces alces shirasi*, known as the Shiras or Wyoming moose, averages 6 feet high at the shoulder and 1,200 pounds for bulls. The animal is found in Wyoming, Idaho, Utah, Montana, and southern British Columbia. A few strays are sometimes seen in Colorado and Washington. Erwin (Joe) Bauer, a well-known outdoor writer and photographer living in Jackson, Wyoming, reports he sometimes can see small herds of moose from his living room window in winter when the rut is over and the animals seek out willow bottoms in the valleys, away from the rigors of high-country weather of the Grand Teton mountains.

The eastern or Canadian moose, *A. a. andersoni*, is larger than its Wyoming cousin and inhabits the dense coniferous forests from Newfoundland westward across the Maritimes to Ontario, and is present in smaller numbers in upper New England. A western moose is found from western Ontario through British Columbia and into the eastern Yukon. Minnesota and Michigan have a few animals, and just recently a moose-hunting season has been proposed for North Dakota, although it is likely to be restricted to residents only.

The largest moose on this continent are found in Alaska. These are the animals that stand over 7 feet tall at the shoulder and may, among bulls, tape up to 9 feet long from nose to stubby tail. *A. a. gigas* bulls can weigh 1,800 pounds and sport massive antlers with great, long antler tines and palms wide enough to serve as a dinner table. In fact, Alaskan moose antlers, if sawed off in one piece and stood on end, can very nearly reach the height of the animal's shoulder—something approaching 6 feet or more.

The Alaska Department of Fish and Game reports that weather, more than any other factor, determines how the state's moose herd will fare. Although moose have legs over 40 inches long, snow much over that depth forces the animals to plow or jump when traveling, and this increases the animal's energy consumption, outstripping the energy intake possible on meager winter rations. Moose surviving a harsh Alaskan winter are in poor condition to reproduce, and calves born to cows in bad shape often fail to live to twelve months of age, the time when most cows drive yearling calves away in preparation for another birth.

From 1956 to 1964, winters were moderate to average and survival was good. In fact, for every 100 cow moose in the state's game-management unit, between forty-two and fifty-five calves were produced each spring, more than doubling the local population. The winter of 1970–71 was very severe, however, and moose mortality reached 50 percent. A direct parallel can be drawn between winter weather and Alaskan moose.

Predation by wolves and brown bears, and to a lesser extent by black bears, also affects moose numbers. A study by Dr. L. David Mech, now with the U.S. Fish and Wildlife Service in Minnesota, on Isle Royale in Lake Superior, determined that wolves there must pursue an average of thirteen moose for every animal pulled down and consumed. And examination of moose kills, including bone marrow tests, showed the great majority of the moose killed and eaten by wolves had been infested with internal parasites and were therefore less able to avoid that fate. Very old and very young moose also fall prey to wolves, and bears sometimes kill newborn calves.

In one southern game unit in Alaska, aerial surveys showed as many as one wolf for every fifteen moose, far more predator pressure than the moose could support. A moose-tagging program conducted in 1973 and 1974, which placed radio-equipped collars on forty moose, showed fully 25 percent of the tagged moose to have fallen to wolves. In 1976, Alaska

Governor Jay Hammond, himself an old wolf hunter and trapper, ignored federal warnings to the contrary and permitted some hunting of wolves from small planes, in an attempt to remove about 80 percent of the wolves in one game unit. The hunts were successful and a number of wolf hides were sold at auction in Anchorage in early 1977. Hammond later relented, however, and stopped future hunts.

Moose breed, or rut in the fall in Alaska, with the peak of the rut occurring in late September and early October. At this time of year the bulls' great antlers have hardened and shed their velvety coverings, and for a time the racks appear starkly white against the darker shades of their habitat. But in short order the bulls begin mock battles with saplings and bushes and this stains the antlers their characteristic brown color. The largest bulls in the state come from the Alaska Peninsula, lower Susitna Valley, and the Kenai Peninsula, with bulls of six to eight years of age producing the greatest trophy antlers. The animals may continue to produce large antlers until they are twelve to fourteen years old, after which the antlers begin to deteriorate. Moose in the wild live slightly more than twenty years.

In Alaska, where much of the moose range is big, open country where vision is good, most hunting is done by glassing open parks, willow forests, and the like, in hopes of spotting big bulls. Since animals are often seen at ranges of well over a mile, a stalk is needed to get closer for a better look and perhaps a shot. Moose do not have exceptional eyesight but they are quick to notice movement. Ears and nose are much better and it's just as important to stalk from downwind on a moose as it is on whitetail deer. Moose antlers can be tough to judge because of the animal's huge body size. Generally, however, a good rack will shade much of the animal's head and neck, and rise well above the ears at their outer edges. Moose antlers, if they are of trophy proportions, can be twice as wide as the bull's chest width.

Rifle calibers for moose are pretty much a matter of personal choice with an eye toward range and wallop. Moose have been dropped in their tracks with very light calibers, but they are heavy-boned animals that, hit in the wrong spot, can absorb a lot of lead. The 7mm Magnum is a good choice when ranges are long, although eastern moose found in dense forest may require a caliber with better brush-busting qualities, such as the .30-06, .300 Winchester Magnum, .338 or .350 Magnum.

Moose hides make thick, tough leather that is especially good for soft shoes because of large pores that permit the leather to "breathe." The Ontario government not long ago instituted a program requesting moose hunters in that province to donate moose hides to the government for distribution among native Indians, who worked the hides into usable items.

Hauling a dead moose, even one cut into quarters, out of dense forest is no job for the weak of heart. More than one hunter, sitting astride his newly fallen trophy, has been faced with the task of quartering and boning nearly half a ton of moose, then toting it many trackless miles to the nearest road or railhead. As one grizzled old guide told me in Ontario, "If you kill a moose back in here, you'd better bring a knife and fork 'cause you'll never get him out."

Moose meat can be delicious, especially if it comes from a young animal or a cow. Bull moose deep in the rut do not eat, but live off the layer of fat they build up in late summer. Feeding resumes in late October following the rut, when the meat again improves. I once sat down to a meal prepared by the Cree wife of a fishing guide in northern Manitoba. The meat dish looked and smelled like beef and was covered with savory brown gravy. It had been a long morning on the lake and we were hungry. The meat was superb—tender, of excellent taste, delicious. Only after the meal did I learn that I had been eating moose; the guide told me each fall he sought out a dry old cow moose for his winter larder. He claimed aged, dry cows make the very best eating, and I would be hard pressed to disagree.

During the rut, bull moose are anything but gregarious beasts. Big, mature bulls move about their range, eating little and seeking out cows ready to mate. Once a cow is located, the bull remains with her for a week to ten days, driving off ambitious yearling bulls and doing full battles with bulls of equal size. The bull then moves on to the next cow he finds, and so forth.

Before and after the rut, however, bulls are much more tolerant of one another, often forming loosely knit herds of ten or more animals. In mountain country, these post-rut bull herds are usually found just above timberline where the new bachelors do not have to compete with cows and calves for the available browse. Lucky is the hunter who finds such a herd, for verily, there must be a trophy head in there somewhere.

Caribou

In the Far North, where time is measured in the wearing away of rock mountains, the vast herds of caribou seem strangely to mesh with the land. For centuries these great herds have moved north and south with the seasons, following the food supplies, the urge to mate and bear calves, the flickers of the northern lights. Their bones have fallen on the tundra of North America for at least 175,000 years, put there by the ever-present threat of tundra wolves, the rigors of winter, the swims across countless arctic rivers and lakes. It is easy to believe that there have always been caribou, and there always will be.

The caribou (*Rangifer tarandus*), known as reindeer in captivity, are thought to be of a single species wherever found throughout the world. And although subspecies are found in such diverse habitat as Alaska's

An average caribou, his wide antlers still in velvet, pauses among the tundra cover to eye an intruder. Caribou have excellent eyesight and hearing but are relatively easy to hunt. (Photo courtesy Alaska Department of Fish and Game)

barren tundra, the high mountain tundra, and the dense fir forests of Canada, where slight differences in body size and color occur, the animal is for the most part about the same.

The Alaskan caribou, the world's only barren ground species, reaches an average weight among bulls of 350 to 400 pounds, although trophies taken in the Aleutians have weighed as much as 700 pounds. Cows average between 175 and 225 pounds. Both bull and cow grow antlers (the world's only deer where this is true), but the cow's antlers are small and thin and are seldom confused with the great, sweeping crown of a mature bull.

The caribou is well adapted to a life in the Far North. Its hooves are wide, often wider than their length, and concave in shape. This allows the hooves to spread a bit when traveling over soft snow or muskeg, and only the outer edges of the hoof touch the ground, leaving a deep, crescent-shaped track.

The hair of the animal is hollow, which helps insulate against arctic cold while making the caribou buoyant while swimming. Its overall ability to pick up and leave an area when the food runs out shows an adaptability not found among other deer.

In late fall caribou are clove-brown with a white rump patch, white neck and feet. The hair of newborn calves is reddish-brown but may range from pale beige to dark brown. The calves weigh about 13 pounds at birth but usually double their weight within two weeks. Within two days the calves can keep up with their mothers, and within ten days they can outrun a man, a definite advantage in country where wolves depend on caribou for food.

After a summer of grazing on southern vegetation in rather small herds, bulls enter the rutting season fat and sleek, often carrying up to 3-inch layers of fat on their backs and hindquarters. Once the rut begins in earnest in October, however, bulls eat little, preferring to expend their energies fighting, gathering herds of a dozen or so cows, and mating. By late October the rut is over, the layer of fat is gone, and the bulls resume feeding. Soon thereafter the bulls begin to shed their magnificent antlers, and most are bald by January.

When the spring migration begins, cows and yearling calves form herds and move to traditional calving areas. In May and June a single calf is born to each cow. Within a few days the newborn calves are fully able to swim lakes and rivers right along with the adults.

In summer, caribou eat a variety of plants, including willow and dwarf birch, grasses, sedges, and succulent plants. As fall moves across the land, the animals switch to lichens (sometimes called reindeer moss) and dried sedges. Wintering caribou can make do with surprisingly short rations, and at that must paw through arctic snow to find it.

At present, there are some 600,000 wild caribou in Alaska, distributed in thirteen distinct herds. Fish and game personnel report the state's western herd has drastically reduced its numbers in recent years due to harsh winters and wolf predation. This can be a real hardship to natives who depend on caribou meat for winter rations. In normal years, about 30,000 caribou are taken by Eskimos and Indians for food and hides.

Two characteristics of barren ground caribou seem strangely out of sync with its harsh, demanding environment. The animal has surprisingly weak eyesight for an animal of open terrain, and this fact has helped many hunters trying to stalk a big bull without the aid of so much as a blade of grass for cover. And although caribou can be spooked by suspicious noises and human scent, they just as often thunder 200 yards away, stop as if trying to remember what scared them in the first place, and then turn around and come trotting back, as if to make sure. They are not overly bright beasts. There are accounts of hunters moving up on watchful herds by stalking on all fours, as a wolf might approach. Why caribou permit wolves to get closer than man is a puzzle, unless they know us better than we think.

Alaska's huge western arctic herd is known to calve in extreme north-

An Alaskan Eskimo dries caribou meat on a makeshift rack. Game meat still provides a major food staple in much of this northern state. (Photo courtesy Alaska Department of Fish and Game)

western Alaska's Brooks Range. It is here, along the headwaters of the Utukok and Colville rivers, the cows come every year to drop their young. Like many herd animals, caribou cows usually bear all young within a short period of time. This means there are several thousand young calves on the ground at the same time, making it virtually impossible for arctic wolves to do real damage to the future of the herd. There is simply too much available prey at one time, and if the wolves pick off even a relatively large number of calves, most will survive those critical first days to assure future caribou numbers. African wildebeests do the same thing, with great success.

As bull caribou mature, their necks become increasingly white, the coloration sometimes spreading over the shoulders. Guides and experienced hunters have learned to look for these spots of white against distant hillsides of dark brown and russet, then deciding if a stalk would be worthwhile. It is not unusual for animals to be spotted from over two miles away in the treeless arctic, and since most stalks are made on foot, the hunter can cover just so much tundra in an afternoon. Sometimes it is wiser to determine the herd's direction of travel, then try to set up an ambush.

Since the modern rifle came to the arctic, even more caribou are being taken by sportsmen and natives alike. David Kaomayok, a fishing guide and Eskimo leader who summers and winters on Victoria Island in the Arctic Ocean, uses a banged-up but serviceable .222 bolt action for all of his hunting, and takes such big game as caribou, musk oxen, and polar bear, not to mention the occasional seal. On the day I visited his camp on Char Lake, David's wife had several dozen strips of caribou meat hung on a drying rack made from the body tubing of an old float plane. The clash of the old and the new made a strange sight indeed.

The caribou is not a tough animal to kill. Its bones are not the massive girders one might find in moose or elk, and it therefore doesn't require the shocking power of a really heavy caliber. Rifles in the .264, .270, and .30-06 range do well in company with bullets of about 130 grains or so. Good bullet design and downrange accuracy are important because many shots are rather long, out to 350 yards in some cases.

Chapter 4

UPLAND BIRDS

Say the words *bird hunting* and what comes to mind depends in large part on where a hunter is from. A downeast New Englander would immediately picture moist cedar bogs, a side-by-side scattergun, and the twittering, twisting flight of a woodcock through a yellow autumn woods. Say it to a Midwesterner and he'll probably reach for his 12-gauge while promising the family they'll have roast of ring-necked pheasant that night. Say *birds* to a gentleman from Georgia or anywhere else in the Deep South and he automatically thinks of Mr. Bob, or pa'tridges, both referring to the bobwhite quail. Mention birds to a wool-jacketed fellow from Michigan or Wisconsin and before you know it a conversation about ruffed grouse has begun. A hunter from New Mexico or Nevada would conjur up thoughts about chukar partridge, while a shirt-sleeved shotgunner from Texas or southern California would get all glassy-eyed with thoughts about whitewinged or mourning dove shooting.

It is obvious that these United States offer a tremendous variety of gamebird shooting. Nearly every part of the nation has one or two species native to the local area where the bird has been hunted for decades, and, predictably, everyone thinks his personal favorite is the toughest to hit, hardest to locate, and best under a knife. Perhaps this is for the best. The hunter fortunate enough to pursue his sport in several sections of the country is treated to fresh enthusiasm wherever he goes, and this leaves no time to become jaded.

Bobwhite Quail

One characteristic of the bobwhite quail is its ability to change its habitat. The covey you've located in a certain fencerow the past five hunting trips, the birds you know will be there every time you go, suddenly aren't present when your pointer gallops by that fencerow without so much as slowing down. They were here yesterday, but where are they today?

It seems that bobwhite quail have changed tactics over the past twenty to thirty years. The birds used to be permanent residents of open weed fields and croplands, visiting heavy cover only when severe weather forced them to temporarily abandon their homes in favor of more protection. Coveys that lived in and around a certain sorghum field or pine woods stayed there, and an experienced local hunter knew where to look for his birds.

Modern bobwhite quail, perhaps in response to increased hunting pressure and a general decrease in the amount and quality of its habitat, has become more and more a creature of big cover—woodlots, honeysuckle tangles, tree nurserys, and the like. Unless hunters happen on a covey during that short period in morning and early evening when the birds are in thin cover while feeding, changes in the bob's lifestyle mean that same hunter had better seek his birds in heavier cover than ever before. Such dense cover is becoming more and more scarce with today's clean-farming practices, and quail in many parts of the country, the Midwest in particular, have declined. But where even minimal cover and food is left, Mr. Bob manages to live and thrive in enough places to keep this handsome little bird among the most popular game species in the country.

Colinus virginianus comes in a variety of subspecies according to where it is found. *C. v. taylori*, commonly found in the Midwest, Oklahoma, and Texas, averages 6 to 7 ounces in weight and up to 10½ inches long from its stubby little fantail to the tip of its strong black bill. Its rounded wings span no more than 15 inches. Other subspecies include *C. v. ridgwayi* of the Sonoran region, which carries a black face; *C. v. floridanus* of Florida's palmetto thickets, which is small and dark; and *C. v. telfanus*, the bobwhite of Texas, which is pale in color.

Quail of all subspecies are hunted in some thirty-five states, making the bird even more popular than the dove for the shotgunner's sport. Wherever found, the bobwhite's lifestyle is about the same.

Bobwhite breed in mid-March in the Deep South, as late as May in the upper Midwest. Cockbirds, bearing the handsome chocolate-brown and white striping on their heads, drop their heads to ground level and fan their wings while rushing at hens in the covey. The hen, if ready to mate, indicates her readiness by turning her back on the cock and refusing to run away. Once mated, the hen's eggs require a gestation period of twenty-three days before a clutch of twelve to fourteen speckled eggs are laid in a small nest sheltered by tall grass and weeds. The hen performs most of the incubation chores during the three weeks it takes before the eggs hatch. Once out into the world, the new quail bear brown

The short, strong wing of a bobwhite quail makes this bird's noisy covey flushes one of the most unnerving among upland birds.

spots on a dull yellow background that help camouflage them in the grass and weeds. From birth until they are nearly full grown, insects form a large part of the quail's diet because of the high protein content. Especially dry springs and summers, which reduce insect life, can be as hard on young quail as cold, rainy springs that drown and chill many birds before they reach full growth.

As late summer and fall approach, insects are replaced by wild and cultivated seeds as the bird's most important diet item, with up to 90 percent of a quail's daily menu consisting of seeds and grain from ragweed, lespedeza, smartweed, beggarweed, soybeans, corn, millet, oats, and wheat. In fact, large cropfields bordered by weeds can be the very best quail habitat, and hunting location, around.

Although bobwhites are among the hardiest of gamebirds, they sometimes suffer from worm infestations, coccidiosis, and enteritis. Severe weather can decimate the quail population. Following the severe winter of 1976–77, considerable numbers of quail were found frozen and starved to death, their crops and stomachs empty because deep, crusted snow

The hard stare of a great horned owl. These and other owls do take occasional gamebirds, especially during late winter, but their diet consists mostly of rodents.

had sealed off all natural foods while preventing the birds from burrowing together for warmth at night.

Deep, persisting snowfall also causes quail death in a manner less direct but no less disastrous. As fencerows and stubble fields become buried under deep snow, the birds are forced to go farther and farther from protective cover in search of food. This makes the covey much more vulnerable to predation by hawks, owls, foxes, housecats, and dogs.

As a quail brood matures in early fall, yearling and adult birds often form very large coveys, sometimes numbering upwards of fifty or more birds. In late autumn, these large groups break up into smaller, more permanent coveys in an annual reorganization called the fall shuffle. These coveys usually number from eight to twenty-five birds and will remain together for the winter, although strays from heavily hunted coveys may join the covey if its own covey is disbanded or falls below six or eight birds due to hunting pressure.

If the bobwhite's summer home also happens to contain good wintering habitat, the birds will move little from season to season. If not, however, quail have been known to move as much as 3 to 4 miles in search of habitat providing good roosting and feeding through the cold months. As winter deepens and temperatures are consistently near freezing at night, quail leave the "edge" cover and move into woodlots, leaving this protection only briefly in morning and evening to feed. Particularly harassed coveys have been known to fly to and from feeding cover, which cuts the chances of predation by wild predators and quail hunters.

Roosting quail spend the nighttime hours in a tight group on the ground, tails together and heads pointed outward in a warm and protective circle where all eyes and ears can detect approaching danger in time to warn all birds in the group. And since quail do not see the sense of getting out of bed to relieve themselves, roosting birds often leave circular "pies" of white droppings where they roost. Knowledgeable hunters keep their eyes peeled for such telltale sign; it is evidence that a quail roosting area has been located.

The first big step in quail hunting is locating the coveys to begin with. Unless there are drastic habitat or weather changes, the birds will be found in the same general vicinity day after day. Look for quail along the edges where food plants border cover plants, such as the edges of cornfields bordering on woods, where an open field of seed-bearing weeds borders a cedar swamp or heavy fencerow. Gone are the days when we could expect to find quail coveys smack in the middle of food plots. They have moved closer to cover as hunting pressure has increased.

There are exceptions, of course. My Brittany spaniel bitch was loafing across a large field of corn stubble one sunny morning. Like me, she knew we seldom found game so far from cover, and like me her mind was elsewhere. I dawdled along behind, my thoughts of the prospects in a far fencerow. Suddenly I missed the dog and stopped to look for her. There she was, some 30 yards behind me, down solid on birds. The covey was at least 100 yards from the nearest cover; inspections of the crops of the two birds I collected from the covey rise indicated they had been eating waste corn. I reasoned the birds had depleted the dropped corn nearer cover and were forced to venture farther than usual from the protective fencerow. On every subsequent trip to that particular field, however, I've found birds in or very near cover, not right out in the field.

Once flushed, bobwhite quail have already decided which direction they will fly, and there is no way you're going to change their minds. If food is available along the edges where light cover meets heavy cover, this is where the birds will be during morning and evening feeding hours. Once flushed off the ground, the birds will head directly back into deep cover, and wise is the hunter who knows this and takes advantage of it.

Let's assume you are using one or more pointing dogs in a large grain field bordered by woods, brushpiles, or other protective cover. The dogs quarter across the field, noses up in the wind, then slow to a crawl before freezing solidly on point not too far from the edge of the field. Beyond the fence is cover. You approach the dogs along an imaginary line from the center of the field toward the fenceline, knowing in advance that the bobs will fly toward the heavier cover. When the covey flushes, hunters approaching along the imaginary line should get straightaway shooting as the birds begin to settle into cover.

Had the hunters approached the dogs and covey from the side, most opportunities would have been passing shots (seldom as good as straightaways). Worse yet, had they walked in on the dogs from the front, the birds would have exploded in their faces, swept past, and required the hunters to spin in their tracks for low-percentage snap shots. Spinning and shooting is a great way to make your hunting companions sweat, I might add.

Keeping your hunting partners' needs and desires in mind while afield is a good way to keep your hunting partners. And that includes never returning to any private place to hunt alone that you first visited as the guest of a friend. That is a serious breach of etiquette that has soured more than one good relationship.

If your nerves are of steel and you are totally incapable of being surprised, by all means try hunting quail without the aid of dogs. When doing so, it's more important than ever to know where to find quail, or you can walk all day and see nothing but field mice and dickey birds. When quail are close, they sometimes make tiny feeding calls, sounding like *tu-tu-tu-tu*. And quail that run from an approaching hunter rather

Whoa now, girl, whoa down. Don't you be pushing those birds out till I get there . . . (Photo courtesy Maine Fish and Game Department)

than immediately taking to wing will often call back and forth to keep the covey together. Both of these sounds can help the dogless hunter, but seldom occur frequently enough to be depended upon.

Someone once compared hunting quail without dogs to running a cow pony in the Kentucky Derby, and I think the analogy a good one. A day afield over a talented pointing dog adds far more than just dead quail to the experience. Quail dogs, be they English pointers, setters, shorthairs, wirehaired pointing griffons, Brittanies, or what have you, know where to look for birds, as well as what cover to ignore. When a large tract is to be hunted, they are the ones searching every trace of scent in the field for birds while the hunter takes the shortest route to the next field. Dogs make the loss of crippled birds a thing of the past, not to mention the sheer enjoyment of watching a graceful pointer race over bird cover, then slam down into a solid point. That's braggin' material.

I bought my first quail dog because I felt guilty about losing wounded birds that had fallen in deep cover and were unretrievable. I chose a Brittany spaniel in order to have the benefits of a good working bird dog, but since that time I've discovered so much more to be gained that I now wonder how I ever did without one. The choices available when buying a hunting dog, and brief outlines on each of the major breeds, are covered in another chapter and I won't elaborate here. I guarantee, though, that you will see more game, collect more fallen game, and more thoroughly enjoy your quail hunting if in the amiable companionship of a dog.

If there ever is a time when good quail dogs are a godsend, it's late in the season when hunting pressure and reduced field cover have driven the bobs into densest cover, be it a brushpile, honeysuckle tangle, or brushy creekbed. Quail are hard enough to hit in open country, and in the woods they become crafty little grouse that put tree trunks between themselves and the shotgun. I want to know where those birds are— exactly where they are—before they flush. A good bird dog can cover a lot of woodland in a short time, and once quail are located the dog points for the hunter who, like me, hates surprises.

A country gentleman I know uses the same shotgun for quail, doves, rabbits, and pheasant. It has been his only shotgun for nearly twenty years and getting him to replace it would be like stealing a grizzly bear cub from its momma. The piece is a 12-gauge pumpgun with a 30-inch full-choke barrel, and it is so worn in places that the metal parts have long since turned dull brown and the fore-end and stock are several shades darker where oil from the human hand has stained it.

The man is at home with this shotgun and, because of the tight choke, can afford to wait out a tight covey flush until the birds are separated in the air and flying in a straight line. I have seen him consistently kill quail at ranges between 35 and 45 yards; he dares not shoot when the birds are much closer because the No. 6 shot and tight choke would blow them apart at shorter ranges. But for all the ease with which this gun serves its owner in the field, it is next to useless in heavy cover or woods. In such places, quail are seldom in sight long enough beyond 20 yards and my friend has had to forego closeup shots while hunters around him were dropping birds.

There certainly is nothing wrong with hunting bobwhites with 12-gauge shotguns, particularly if that's the only gun you own. But if two shotguns are not beyond your means, then do obtain a 20-gauge bored skeet or improved cylinder. The bob is a light-skinned, fragile little bird and today's

*The red fox has a varied diet that in-
cludes the odd rabbit or gamebird, but
not enough to greatly alter local game
populations.*

20s pack more than enough wallop to kill quail efficiently and cleanly.

My favorite quail gun is a featherweight 20-gauge over-and-under double-barrel bored skeet up and down. It weighs less than 6 pounds and since both barrels are choked (or not choked) identically, switching from one barrel to another isn't necessary. I prefer skeet loads (low base, quick expanding) with shot sizes from 7½ to 9. Shot this small permits a dense pattern at short ranges, those I encounter most often when hunting quail over a dog. The over-and-under style offers a single sighting plane, and I just like the heft and feel of it. Because it is so light, the shotgun swings fast, important when hunting birds in tight cover.

Single-shot scatterguns may be used on quail, of course. They too are light, and their one-shot-only configuration is especially advisable for youngsters just learning the shooting sports. They are limited to just one pop at fast-disappearing quail, however.

Pump-operated shotguns, one of the most popular styles, come in all gauges and weights and give the shooter up to five shots, although many gunners restrict their loadings to three shells.

Semiautomatic shotguns eliminate the need to manually jack fresh rounds into firing position when that covey is already 25 yards out and fading fast. The semis also are available in some featherweight models, which cut toting weight by as much as 2 pounds. Gas-operated models reduce the shotgun's kick because some of the force released when shells are fired is used to activate the reloading mechanism. I should add, for the benefit of other left-handers like myself, that too few firearms manufacturers see the need to produce semiautomatic shotguns with the gas ports located on the left side of the shotgun. This leaves us portsiders putting up with possible powder blasts on our cheeks, or the option of choosing some other style of quail gun.

Ring-necked Pheasant

In many parts of the country, pheasant hunting isn't what it once was. Time was when a man and his dog could take a late breakfast in Iowa, Illinois, the Dakotas, Nebraska, or Ohio, slip out to the back forty for an hour or so, and come home two hours before lunch with a limit of two birds with no trouble at all. And he'd probably have seen half a dozen other roosters and a dozen hens after that number-two bird added weight to his pocket. Farms were small, farm machinery still depended on two-mule power, and a farmer didn't feel the need to hide his face if his neighbors saw fallow fields and overgrown brush along the fences. Pesticides and granulated fertilizers had yet to become popular, and plenty of wild seed-bearing weeds were around where a cockbird and his harem could nest and raise a family without worrying too much about a county tank truck wetting them down with weed killer.

The flat cornland of central Ohio once held so many wild pheasant

Where both cocks and hens can be hunted, ring-necked pheasant can provide very good shooting. These birds came from federal lands stocked with pen-raised birds.

that hunters with a free weekend traveled there from New York and even the West Coast for a few days of fine shooting. I can remember coveys of ringnecks getting airborne at the same time along winding Rattlesnake Creek, so rattling a greenhorn kid with his single-shot scattergun that when the smoke had cleared and the birds gone, nary a one graced the grass at his feet. I've seen flocks of pheasant unconcernedly pecking their way from one end of a Midwestern beanfield to another, looking like so many wild chickens.

Well, those days are gone, and with them the pheasant. We turned the corner in the early 1940s with gasoline-powered farm machinery, elimination of the 100-acre farm, and the combination of greed and embarrassment that won't allow a farmer to do less than intensively farm every square inch of dirt on the place.

The history of the Chinese ring-necked pheasant (*Phasianus colchicus*) in the United States fits all the stereotypes of the immigrant-makes-good stories. Until 1881, those few pheasant brought to this country were meant for immediate shooting sport. But in 1881, a shipment of ringnecks was made to Corvallis, Oregon, by Owen H. Denny, consul-general at Shanghai, China. The birds were released on the farm of Denny's brother and within a decade offspring of the original twenty-one birds had spread throughout the Willamette Valley. Soon after, other plantings were made in at least ten states. In the next fifty years, more plantings took place, some of them including strains of European and Japanese birds, to develop the hardy and aggressive bird we know today. For once, those who get their kicks by moving wildlife from one part of the world to another had a success they could point to.

To American hunters used to bobwhite quail, woodcock, and grouse, the ringneck was a harsh teacher in reality. Where the other gamebirds sat politely under a point, stayed put in certain cover, and hardly ever ran away, the ringneck started breaking rules. This was a bird of the wide-open spaces—cornfields, wheatfields so big they got hazy blue in the distance, and rolling, open woodlands. No dummy at survival, the pheasant not only outwitted hunter and dog, but actually seemed to laugh aloud about it with a parting cackle.

The American hunter had to develop a different way of hunting to score with any consistency on this big, gaudy intruder from the Far East. He was the new guy in town, tough, resourceful, dynamically opposed to doing what you thought he would do, and unforgiving when the hunter made mistakes. We learned to love him, but only as we love a wealthy mother-in-law.

If the cock ringneck isn't the most handsome bird in North America, he is certainly the gaudiest gamebird. The head and neck are colored an iridescent green with hints of violet and blue when the light hits it a glancing blow. The yellow eye is widely surrounded by a red patch, giving the bird the appearance of a wild chicken (occasionally one will see an all-white pheasant—which looks all the more like a chicken!). Low ear tufts, longer on some specimens than others, grace the top rear of the head. A neat, white border ring of color separates the green of the head and neck from a body covered with scalelike feathers in patterns of brown, russet, and copper, and the base of the long, flowing tail bears tiny hackle feathers of light blue. Wing coverts have light tan feathers with brown borders, and the flight feathers are a dull gray-brown with darker bars. The legs and feet are near-black; two-year-old cocks often wear inch-long spurs, and all pheasant have long scratching claws on all four toes of each foot.

The hen pheasant is much more drab than her mate, undoubtedly to afford her camouflage protection while brooding her nest. The hen's neck and body also contain scaled feathers but the entire bird is a uniform brown, and the female's tail feathers are much shorter than the male's. The hen is considerably less wary, often preferring to remain hidden in deep grass when man approaches while the more easily spooked cock has long since made tracks.

The wild cock pheasant in good health will weigh from 2½ to 4 pounds; the hen will weigh from 1½ to 3 pounds. Pen-raised pheasant meant for commercial shooting preserves get plenty of corn and other high-protein rations and can exceed 5 pounds in weight. Such added weight often slows the bird's flush and level flight, however.

Unlike the bobwhite, pheasant haven't changed tactics much in the

A plump hen pheasant leaves the sparse cover of late-winter weeds and leaps into a flush. Where legal, hen pheasant add a lot of shooting, although rooster pheasant are preferred by a good many hunters.

past fifty years. They haven't had to—they were tough enough in the beginning and they haven't gotten any easier. For man and dog alike, pheasant require perseverance, a lot of hiking, not a little cunning, and the discipline to ignore the fact that a flushing pheasant looks as big as a turkey. As Charlie Waterman writes in the fine book edited by Robert Elman and George Peper, *Hunting America's Game Animals & Birds*

This pair of pen-raised pheasant will be stocked on a commercial shooting preserve. Such preserves offer up to eight months of shooting for a price.

(Winchester Press, 1975), "Watch a cock pheasant coming for a hundred yards, track him with the muzzle, take great care to do everything just right, and you'll miss him sure as hell." Most ringneck hunters have had the humbling experience of shooting at the entire bird at close range, and ending up doing nothing more than perforating a few tail feathers. A pheasant on the rise probably moves no faster than 20 miles per hour, but once it shifts gears and begins level flight, it can move at speeds approaching 50 miles per hour, especially with a tail wind. No wonder we miss.

Firearms used for pheasant cover the spectrum from 20- to 12-gauges, but the 12 is easily the most popular choice. Its greater punch is often needed on this big, tough bird with feathers that sometimes seem to shed lead shot like rhinoceros hide. A solid body hit is probably the easiest and surest place to kill a ringneck, although a few times I have put a bird on the grass with a single No. 6 shot in the head. Unintentionally, let me hasten to add. Hunters owe it to the bird to score on as many of their shots as possible. Pheasant are hardy and a wounded bird still able to run will do just that, eluding even excellent dogs while it hides under a brushpile or down a groundhog burrow. It may die later, uncollected by the hunter, food for the foxes and crows.

The most popular pheasant loads are probably tossups between No. 4 and No. 6 shot. Both hold their velocity well out of full-choke or modified tubes, the only logical barrel choices for this big, fast bird.

Although the pheasant sometimes retreats to woodlands, lowland cattail thickets, and the like during extreme weather or to relieve hunting pressure, it is mainly a bird of the open fields, fencerows, and brushy drainage ditches. After a light snow, or when the earth is soft after a rain, look for the bird's distinctive crosslike tracks along fences, in picked and standing corn, around brushy water holes, and in and around islands of heavy uncut weeds. Discovering fresh tracks tells you there are birds in the immediate vicinity—but you can't eat tracks.

Once you've established there are birds about, there are two basic hunting methods—with and without bird dogs. Hunting without dogs is pretty much like a deer drive, with a field selected, standers and drivers placed, and the birds (hopefully) urged to run ahead of the drivers until they come out of cover and flush for the standing guns. ("Cover" to a sneaky cock pheasant is anything taller than bare earth; they can hide under the yellow line on a highway.)

Standers should be placed along any slackening in the cover—plowed earth, barren fencerow, gravel road, whatever. Running pheasant are reluctant to cross coverless ground and should flush for the standers. Drivers need not make a great deal of noise—the birds will already know they aren't alone in the field—and the line of drivers should contain spaces between drivers of no more than 15 yards, lest the birds dodge behind the line. The drivers on each end of the line should position themselves slightly ahead of the center drivers, forming a sort of moving cup that keeps birds from making an end run to freedom.

The lone driver stands little chance of seeing many pheasant because the birds merely step out of his path in deep cover and he never knows the bird was anywhere close. He can do well with just one good bird dog, however. The dog covers a lot more ground than a hunter alone, can detect birds at far greater distances because of scent on the wind, and, with a little experience, can pin run-crazy pheasant under a point until the hunter puffs up.

Any bird dog that gets birds for his handler is worthy of being called a "pheasant dog," but some are better than others. The good ones can be separated into two groups, the flushers and the pointers. Flushing dogs scramble directly after a fleeing pheasant until it flushes, hopefully within gun range. The two most popular breeds of flushing dogs for pheasant are Labrador retrievers and English springer spaniels. Both can be pure joy to share a day afield with, being amiable, talented, and enthusiastic, and well-schooled individuals are responsive to commands.

Flushing dogs should hunt for the hunter, not in spite of him, be responsive to commands, stay within reasonable range, be bold on the flush, and do a credible job of tracking and retrieving. The finer points of selecting, training, and keeping hunting dogs are covered in detail in another chapter.

Pointing breeds offer more variety from which to choose. The wide-ranging breeds (dog men call them big runners) would include English pointers and setters, while medium-range dogs include the German short-hair pointers, German wirehair pointers, plus the keen little Brittany spaniels for those who like their dogs to hunt close to the gun.

A useful pointing pheasant dog should do at least three things: range wide enough to cover a healthy chunk of real estate so the hunter doesn't have to; have the ability and common sense to be able to wind a pheasant skulking several dozen yards upwind and move in on the bird; and be mobile enough on point to keep that bird's belly to the ground until the hunter flushes it.

Unlike doves or woodcock, you don't just shoot pheasant. You hunt them. And may this never change.

Ruffed Grouse

The wooded ridges and sidehills I hunt for ruffed grouse contain a lot of birds. They are fine sport, lifting off with roaring wings and a brown blur designed to thrill the most jaded hunter. But those same hills are proof positive that God never let man have things entirely his own way, and all because of a terrible little thorny plant called greenbrier. The greenbrier grows close to the ground in dense patches and seems to have been put on this earth for the sole purpose of grabbing, tangling,

The ruffed grouse is considered king of the gamebirds in much of the Northeast and Upper Midwest. Seasons are long and daily bag limits average three per hunter. (Photo courtesy U.S. Fish and Wildlife Service)

and otherwise fouling the boots worn by grouse hunters. Whenever I walk up on a grouse dog all quivering and staunch on point, my feet become befouled in greenbrier, which ruins my concentration and I miss the shot. If it weren't for greenbrier, I'm convinced I'd be the best grouse shot in the state.

The reddish-brown little woods bird is known as the ruffed grouse because of the jaunty ruff of feathers atop the bird's head. This bird, which weighs no more than 1¼ pounds soaking wet, flies at about 25 miles per hour in dense cover and less than twice that in the open. The grouse is found over much of the eastern half of the United States, plus northern California, the lower Canadian provinces, and central Alaska. Its range extends as far south as Tennessee and northern Georgia. The best hunting in terms of grouse populations is found in New England, the upper Great Lakes, the middle Rockies, and the forested mountains of the Pacific Northwest.

Although there are a minimum of eleven subspecies of ruffed grouse, two are most common. In southern Canada and the Rockies, the gray-feathered phase (*Bonasa umbellus umbelloides*) is most often found at higher elevations than its red counterpart, and is slightly larger. The red phase (*B. u. umbellus*), most frequently found in the East and Midwest, bears reddish-brown plumage designed to blend with the leafy forest floor of its deciduous home.

The dog has a right to be proud of his hunter's three-grouse limit. Grouse don't sit well under a point and must be carefully handled by pointing dogs. (Photo courtesy Peter and Stephen Maslowski)

Although grouse country often covers many square miles of woodland, hills, and open, brushy parks, the species seems to favor certain coverts year after year. They also show a definite preference for certain types of cover in various extreme weather situations. In grouse country, it's always a good bet to check old abandoned farms, where pasturelands are in the process of returning to the wild state. Such spots are usually full of bud and fruit-bearing trees, shrubs, and bushes that attract grouse. Seldom will many birds be found in tall, mature forest, simply because the dense overstory (leafy tree growth) cuts off sunlight to the forest floor and thereby inhibits growth by food-bearing plants. Specific foods eaten by grouse include aspen buds, wild grapes, acorns, beechnuts, serviceberry, blackberries, hornbeam, and greenbrier. Wherever the grouse is found, it is never far from dense cover, especially at first light and late in the evening. Grouse prefer to roost for the night in coniferous stands because such spots offer dense protection from night-hunting owls and good insulation against snow and rainfall. Hunters often spot grouse perched on overhead limbs from which the birds tilt their heads from side to side, peer down at the hapless hunter, and perhaps even refuse to fly if a handy pine cone is chucked their way. And some hunters have no qualms about popping unwary birds perched in trees or frozen stock-still on the ground, saying they're sure any advantage they can get on grouse is little enough to salve the pain of past misses. To do this is to deny the grouse its major contribution to the upland gunner's sport. The bird is *supposed* to scare the hell out of you when it flushes.

A good grouse gun is any shotgun short enough to handle well in tight cover, light enough to be toted uphill and down all day long, open choked enough to throw a wide pattern at short ranges, and capable of holding at least two shots in case you want to celebrate a clean miss by firing a shot in the air.

I use the same gun for grouse, quail, and woodcock, a light over-and-under 20-gauge bored skeet up and down. I load it with low-base skeet loads designed to open the pattern quickly, and I shoot No. 9 or No. 9½ shot because such loads are very dense, open up quickly, and pack enough punch to put the fragile grouse to beating its death drum, provided I can hit the bird in the first place. Once down, grouse have the habit of flapping their wings against dried leaves, sticks, or whatever they land on, making things much easier for dog or man in search of a downed bird.

If you use dogs for grouse hunting, choose a close-working dog with enough light coloration in its coat to be easily seen in dark woods. Clip a small bell to its collar so you'll know the dog is on a bird, when the tink-tink-tink stops. Pick a dog that, once down on point, won't move an eyelash no matter what the bird does. Grouse are nervous under a dog's glare, and the dog that cheats or creeps up on an already pointed bird will push it into flight before you're ready. Retrievers and flushers have also been used for Mr. Ruff with good success, and these include the Labrador and golden retrievers, English springers, and even the odd cocker with a nose for bird scent. English setters and the Gordons are excellent grouse dogs. A few red-coated Irish setters are still used as downeast grouse and woodcock dogs. The Brittany, a close worker with good bird sense, is a fine grouse choice.

Woodcock

The American woodcock may well be the most beautifully adapted bird on the continent. It has shortened legs, presumably so it can more easily plunge its 2½-inch bill into soft earth seeking earthworms. Its eyes have moved from the middle of its head to a point closer to the top of its head, the better to remain alert while plunging for worms. This in turn forced its brain to a spot where no other bird carries its brain—far back in the head and upside down in the bargain. Its supersensitive bill can "taste" worms in the ground and has a uniquely hinged feature for grabbing them before they can burrow away. To top it off, the woodcock is a shore bird that no longer lives on the shore and has rounded, stubby wings ill-suited for the long-distance fall and spring migration flights it makes every year. Other than this, there is nothing remarkable about the woodcock.

Philohela minor nests from eastern Minnesota into Michigan and eastward through New Brunswick, Nova Scotia, and Maine. A smaller breeding population exists in Ohio, lower New England, and West Virginia. Fall migrations covering up to 1,500 miles find the birds wintering in Florida, Louisiana, and Central America. Harvest for the woodcock, like those for migratory doves and waterfowl, is controlled by the federal government, when flight birds (migrants) mix with local populations. In most of its range, the woodcock season opens in early to mid-October and runs through mid- to late November. Louisiana is its major wintering ground in the United States; hunting begins there in December and ends in February.

Knowing that the woodcock eats worms as its chief menu item should tip the hunter about where to look for birds. Lowland woods are always a good bet, since they contain terrain with enough natural ground moisture to attract and hold worms and with enough overhead foliage to retard the sun's dehydration. Light woodlands, consisting chiefly of thumb-size water oaks or other bottomland trees, hold birds during the fall flights. Just when the birds will arrive from up north is subject to a few days' variation, but generally the migration must keep ahead of the frost and freeze line of late fall if the birds are to find enough earthworms on their way south.

Feeding woodcock leave telltale signs for the hunter knowing what to look for. Pencil-diameter bore holes, left when the bird plunges its bill into the earth in search of worms, is a dead giveaway. Another sign, usually found in the same spots, is bird droppings.

The timberdoodle is a bird that loves the edges of light woods and meadows and where upland field meets the moister bottomlands. There is a tiny, meandering creek within two miles of my home. Whenever a perfect October afternoon comes along, I always find a dozen or so plump flight birds refueling for a day or so along that tiny brook before heading on south. My Brittany, delighted at this chance for some early bird work, snuffles her way between the maples toward the creek. Within

The woodcock's brown, white, and tan plumage make it nearly impossible to see against the forest floor. These little birds sit well under a point. (Photo courtesy Maine Fish and Game Department)

moments I notice that the spaniel's footfalls have stopped and I look about. There, as solid as if painted in canvas, the dog has a bird pinned against a sassafras trunk.

It is sometimes predictable where a woodcock will head. The bird will seek some flying room, and that means rising through overhead leaves into the nearest patch of sunlight. I gamble that this pattern will hold consistent this time, circle a bit to the right, and step in to jump the bird.

The little brownish-black bird is suddenly visible as it flutters quickly off the carpet of leaves, its primaries making the distinctive twittering sound. Sure enough, the bird heads for the nearest open spot and my load of 9s catches it just before it shifts gears into level flight. The bird falls softly to the ground and my dog, showing utter distaste for the task, picks up the bird by the tip of one wing and walks back with it, as if retrieving woodcock was not her idea of something to do.

If you shoot at a woodcock and miss, watch its flight path carefully. Woodcock don't fly far when flushed and it's possible to relocate the same bird several times, provided you miss it that much. When flight birds are in (they usually travel at dusk), coverts that contained only a handful of birds one day may hold ten times that many the next day. A tight-working dog can then be extremely important if the dog is to avoid bumping a second bird while working the first.

Doves

It is just before four in the afternoon on a hot September afternoon. You are seated uncomfortably on a knotty fallen log in a patch of tall foxtail weeds bordering a field of newly picked corn. The beads of sweat that have darkened the underside of your camouflage-colored hat form a trickle that runs inside your collar and down your chest and you wonder if you shouldn't head for home and a cold beer or two.

The sweat has been smeared away for the twenty-fifth time when two black specks appear over the far treeline; you watch them idly for a few moments, then, forgetting the heat, lean forward on your knotty perch and finger the safety on your shotgun. The birds are nearer now, and closing. They're doves—pointed wings beating quickly, tapering tails straight out behind, and the telltale rounded heads. As the birds fly within 25 yards you jump to your feet, jerk the 12-gauge to cheek, and fire. The first bird does a complete roll without breaking stride and for a moment you think the shot went home, but just as quickly the bird levels out, does another snap roll for good measure, and is gone behind the treeline. Then a lone dove sneaks through the trees on your left, zips to ground level, and flutters in to feed less than 50 feet away. You wipe away more sweat, jack another round into the shotgun, and hope the feeding bird chokes on its meal. Later you'll tell friends how much you enjoy a good dove shoot.

That's the way dove shooting is for most of us, whether our bird is whitewing (*Zenaida asiatica*) or mourning dove (*Zenaidura macroura carolinensis*). Far more doves are shot at than are killed by hunters every year, and far more doves die of natural causes annually than ever hear the sound of a shotgun at all. In fact, if America's ammunition manufacturers were ever to adopt a mascot, it would undoubtedly be the dove. Dove hunters use more ammunition in the pursuit of their sport than all the world's grouse hunters would consume in fifty lifetimes. And they undoubtedly come home with less to show for their efforts.

The mourning dove, also known as turtle dove, rain crow, and Carolina dove, is this country's most plentiful dove. Said to contain the largest population east of the Mississippi River, Ohio boasts an estimated 7.4 million doves every year. Similar populations can be found along the lower Atlantic Coast, throughout the Deep South, and in decreasing density all the way to California. The bird itself measures about a foot from the tip of its tapered tail to its pointed black bill. Graceful wings span 20 inches from tip to tip, and the overall coloration is a soft gray, with primary feathers, a few side spots, and a distinctive cheek spot somewhat darker. The belly is a creamy white and the legs and feet are bright red. Mature doves (males) carry an iridescent sheen on the neck area.

The normal cruising speed for doves trading between feeding, roosting, and watering areas is about 35 miles per hour, but birds with a tail wind, perhaps one dusted with shot, can speed up to 60 miles per

The dove's long, slender body lends itself to fast, acrobatic flight, a fact most dove hunters can swear to (and often do). (Photo courtesy Karl H. Maslowski)

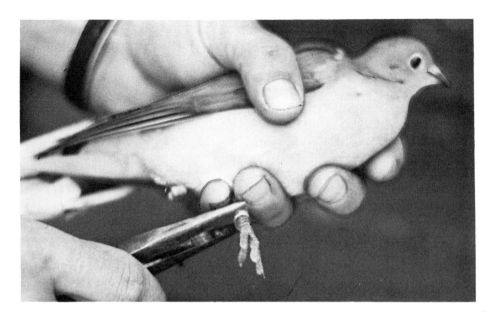

Banding programs have shown mourning doves to suffer annual losses approaching 80 percent, regardless of whether they are hunted or not. They succumb to freezing and starvation.

hour and be out of range before your first hull hits the stubble. The species is capable of a full range of aerobatics, and these birds think it no trick at all to literally dodge a shotload in midair.

In some states, spring nesting begins as early as March. A mated pair constructs a primitive and shaky platform nest of twigs, with coniferous trees the preferred nesting site. Two eggs are laid, and within two weeks of hatching the young are abandoned when the adults set about readying for their next brood. Up to half-a-dozen broods may be produced in a single summer. Nestlings are fed a unique, pastelike substance called "pigeon milk," which the adults regurgitate on demand by the young.

As with all wildlife species with a high reproductive rate, most doves do not live to reach their first birthday. From 65 to 80 percent of all doves die, most from natural causes, in their first year. Drought, prolonged cold or rainfall, predator thievery of eggs, and nest destruction by wind keep the average dove population about the same year after year. This is true whether the birds are hunted or not, although those opposing dove hunting adamantly refuse to believe this.

In fact, states with established dove-hunting seasons are likely to increase their average dove population by creating habitat particularly favoring the species, such as fields of cultivated grain, foxtail, millet, and the like. Not only that, but the tremendous volume of shotgun shells purchased every fall by dove hunters provides a huge sum in the form of excise tax on sporting arms and ammunition specifically earmarked for wildlife management and related programs. All in all, then, the dove is a well-nigh perfect gamebird.

Newcomers to dove hunting are surprised to learn that the sport actually involves very little real *hunting.* The only hunting is finding a location where doves are likely to fly within range. Thereafter it becomes dove *shooting*, provided you can hit the targets.

In the South, where grand social events have been built around group dove hunts for many decades, the event might start off with a barbeque lunch and a tub of cold beer. After the last chicken leg and frosty can have been consumed, the hunters carry shotguns, shell sacks, and comfortable camp stools to a predetermined shooting field known to attract flights come to feed on waste grain. The hunters spread around the edges of the field, some in the welcome shade of a treeline, others right out in the open, sitting in plain sight. The first few birds to appear over the field are followed from one end to the other by shooting as everyone gets into the act. Perhaps one shooter, displaying early luck, dusts the bird's feathers with a load of No. 7s, or perhaps all the shooting doesn't change the dove's mind and it settles in the middle of the field and begins to peck for grain, totally oblivious to the activity around it. More birds—dozens of them—will zip over the shooters before quitting time about 7 P.M.

In the North and West, dove hunting is a bit less social and matches local conditions. In some states a gravel pit or millet field might be the site, while in Arizona a handful of hunters crouch near cacti around a water hole in wait of the slightly smaller whitewings.

As the hunting season (set by federal guidelines) progresses, the birds become warier and the average number of shells expended per dove gets larger and larger. In most states, the dove season is split into two or even three parts, beginning in early September and finally ending as late as January. Hunters welcome this system because the forced closure of hunting between segments gives the birds time to calm down, and it gives hunters a chance to raid local gun shops for a couple more cases of shells. Shotguns used for doves, both whitewings and mourning doves, go all the way from vintage old twelves with taped fore-ends, to gas-operated autos with vent ribs. All gauges, from 28s through 12s, do the job. What's probably most important in any dove gun is the barrel constriction. Early in the season, before doves have had enough shooting to become flighty and high-flying, open-choked guns are best because the birds are likely to fly close to the gun. Later, when the now-wary birds are trading back and forth at considerable altitude, modified or even full-choke barrels will dust the most birds. Shot from 6s to 9s is used.

But no choke and no shotgun, no matter how perfect, will kill a dove unless the hunter's lead was right to begin with. An old-timer in Kentucky once told me, as an instruction about how to hit doves, "Take a much longer lead than you think is necessary, and double that. Then double it again. Then *maybe* you'll hit more than the tail feathers."

I once took a friend on his first dove shoot. Amazingly, he hit the first seven birds he shot at, then missed at least the next dozen in a row and never did fill his twelve-bird limit. He said at least eight of those doves flew away and over the trees following his shots, stone-dead without knowing it.

Here's a tip for some really super early-season dove shooting, at least in terms of the huge numbers of birds it can bring. Before the season opens check with local farmers or a county agricultural agent to find out which grain farmers in your region usually harvest crops sooner than their neighbors. Then knock on some farmhouse doors and get permission to hunt the newly harvested field. Harvesting by modern methods leaves a large amount of fallen grain in the field, and somehow word gets around quickly. Within forty-eight hours that field will be visited regularly by what you'll swear is every dove in five states, all cashing in on the newly available grain. The birds spread their feeding to more and more farms as grain crops continue to be harvested.

Besides a shotgun, the dove hunter needs very little equipment. Some hunters wear camouflage clothing and even face masks, but many do well in dark-colored shirts. Folding camp stools with a canvas game pocket keep the hunter comfortable on stand and do a nice job of carrying extra shells. A plain mesh potato sack is excellent for carrying birds until they can be cleaned and put on ice. Some hunters owning bird dogs and retrievers put their dogs to work fetching doves from deep cover, an excellent conservation measure. Dove feathers come out easily, however, and some dogs dislike getting a mouthful of tickle every time they retrieve a fallen bird.

If you are truly gung-ho, you can make plywood or heavy cardboard cutouts resembling perched doves, adding coathanger wire stands. These should be posted in dead, leafless trees in fencerows, along wire fences, or upright around mud-banked water holes. Doves will decoy much like waterfowl, and I've had live doves sit down smack in the middle of my decoys and coo contentedly even though the chap on the left didn't coo in return. Doves are fast, but they aren't the most intelligent creatures God ever created.

Chapter 5

WATERFOWL

About twelve million ducks fall as a result of hunting activity every year in the United States. Of these, a bit more than ten million are killed and bagged by hunters. The remainder die from lead poisoning after eating spent shot pellets. Lead poisoning of waterfowl affects both the game itself and the way we hunt it.

It is remarkable that waterfowl can be reduced so considerably every fall in all four of this nation's flyways, only to return in about the same numbers a year later. They are a truly renewable resource that should continue to provide superb sport for generations, given proper and intelligent management.

Lead vs. Steel

Lead poisoning as a danger to waterfowl is not new. It was recognized as a mortality factor in North America as early as 1874. This first report came from Texas. Similar reports on lead's effects on ducks, geese, and swans came from Currituck Sound, North Carolina, in 1901, and from Puget Sound, Washington, in 1908. Other reports about the problem came from Virginia, Michigan, Illinois, Ohio, and Wisconsin in the years following those initial reports. Many reports detailed only the symptoms of the problem: waterfowl appearing to be undernourished and unable to fly or swim or even walk normally on dry land. Dead ducks were gathered and examined and found to have large quantities of undigested grain in their gizzards, so the problem was obviously not one of simple starvation.

In 1960 the Mississippi Flyway Council, consisting of state fish and game departments from Minnesota, Wisconsin, Michigan, Ohio, Indiana,

Comfortable to all except for the cold, a pair of big-water hunters get set to fire at some passing birds. (Photo courtesy Michigan Tourist Council)

Illinois, Iowa, Missouri, Arkansas, Kentucky, Tennessee, Alabama, Mississippi, and Louisiana, began working closely with the U.S. Fish and Wildlife Service (FWS) on the lead-poisoning problem. In fact it was this council that initiated the intensive research on lead shot ingestion and waterfowl mortality for the past seventeen years.

The Mississippi Flyway includes fourteen states, one-fourth of the area within the continental United States. Within this area are found a quarter of the nation's waterfowl and one-third of its human population. Of the flyway's 56 percent of this country's high-value waterfowl habitat, fully 2.5 million acres lie within some 5,000 private duck-club boundaries. Forty percent of this country's duck hunters (664,000 gunners) pursue their sport within the flyway states. With this type of credentials, the

Mississippi Flyway was in an excellent position to determine the problem and work on possible solutions.

From all over the flyway came reports of "starving" waterfowl, in some cases moving local residents to spread shelled corn around the marshes for the ducks. But with or without the supplemental feedings, waterfowl deaths continued to occur. Just how serious the problem had become was made known in a 1959 report that said that between 5 and 10 percent of the ruddy ducks, mallard, blacks, and pintails were ingesting lead shot pellets, and more than 10 percent of the canvasbacks, scaup, red-heads, and ring-necked ducks were infected. The problem had suddenly become serious with these revelations.

Not all waterfowl that eat lead pellets die, but even a single No. 6 lead pellet is fatal in 9 percent of the cases. Two pellets will kill about one-fourth of the ducks, and chances for survival are less than 50 percent. Even the mallard, this continent's most important sporting species of duck, is in the middle of this problem. Mallard are reported to make up a considerable portion of the annual die-off of two million lead-poisoned ducks; a full fourth of the mallard population ingests lead shot each year, and 4 percent of the mallard in North America die in the wild from lead poisoning. Put another way, poisoning took as many mallard as Mississippi Flyway hunters legally bagged in 1961 and 1962. That is a *lot* of ducks.

Lead pellets that are picked up by a feeding duck settle in the bird's gizzard where normal muscular contractions peel tiny lead flakes away from the pellets. The flakes are then absorbed into the duck's bloodstream through the digestive tract, and typical lead-poisoning symptoms soon become apparent. The gizzard suffers paralysis; the gizzard's muscular walls can no longer grind grains and seeds for digestion. This explains why a duck appearing to be starved and emaciated may have a gizzard full of corn—the grain goes that far and stops, offering no nourishment.

A bird suffering from lead poisoning loses weight and becomes weak; increased paralysis results as the loss of nerve response spreads to other body muscles. The bird can no longer fly and it paddles over the water surface in a clumsy manner. In the final stages, the bird can no longer walk on land or even hold its head erect. The bird is eventually found dead on the marsh or lakeshore.

Autopsies performed on lead-poisoned waterfowl show considerable internal damage. Enlargement of the liver, kidneys, and spleen is apparent, and tests showed that lead fragments stored in bone tissue may be slowly released to destroy the heart and liver. Hen mallard that had suffered lead poisoning produced fewer eggs than did others that had never suffered the malady.

Spent lead pellets are usually available to waterfowl anywhere wetland hunting is an annual activity. One Missouri public shooting area manager reported that two hunters require 288 shells to bag their eight-duck limit;

this amounted to thirty-six shots per duck. On Wisconsin's Horicon Marsh, twenty-three shots were estimated for each goose taken. On Michigan's Swan Creek Public Shooting Area, a five-year average of sixty-eight shells for every goose bagged, and a one-year high of eighty-four shots per bird taken, show just how plentiful is the spent lead. One Ohio study showed a total of 25,391 rounds of shotgun ammunition fired

Hip boots are a way of life for the dedicated waterfowler. Without them, many ducks could not be located.

at waterfowl represented 31,739 ounces of lead, nearly a *ton of shot.* This is an awful lot of potential waterfowl poison.

Certainly, not all spent shot is readily available to feeding waterfowl. Availability depends on the amount of shooting over a particular wetland, firmness of the bottom, water depth, siltation rate, and the amount of ice cover. Some hunting hotspots seem specially suited to making shot available to feeding birds; a 1916 study by Alexander Wetmore, who examined mud samples around two duck blinds at the mouth of the Bear River in Utah, found up to twenty-two pellets per sample, enough to poison thousands of feeding ducks. This was the first lead-poisoning study ever made in the country.

Short of a complete ban on waterfowl hunting, what was needed was a replacement for the toxic lead shot, but what? A study conducted at the Winchester Group's Nilo Farms at Alton, Illinois, tested lead, iron, and copper shot under tightly controlled conditions to determine the various characteristics of the three metals. Some 2,400 pen-raised mallard were shot at varying ranges with steel, lead, and copper pellets, using Nos. 4 and 6 steel, No. 4 pure copper, and No. 4 lead shot.

Test mallard were attached to a special transport device that was electrically driven down a 100-foot track. Limit switches tripped an electronic timer and the solenoid that fired a full-choke 12-gauge shotgun; the gun was clamped in a rigid mount at ranges of 30, 40, 50, 60, 70, and 80 yards. All variables such as wind drift of shot, temperature, wind velocity and direction, speed of the transport device, and other factors were monitored.

After being fired on, living birds were tested for coordination. Ten days later, after being held in pens with food and water, the birds were tested for flying ability and all were ultimately classed as bagged, crippled, or survivors. The birds were then sent to the University of Wisconsin where they were fluoroscoped to check broken bones and locations of embedded pellets; in addition, some 480 ducks were completely defeathered to determine entrance and exit wounds and pellet penetration.

The test determined that a shotshell's effectiveness on waterfowl depends on three factors: striking energy of each pellet, the efficiency with which the pellet delivers its energy, and the number of pellets striking the bird's vital areas.

Lead, steel, and copper pellets of the same size were found to be similar in efficiency of energy delivery and in the number of pellets striking vital areas. However, the pellet's striking energy was about proportional to the density of the shot metal used.

Only at the 30-yard range were the four shotshells used found to be comparable. At 40 yards, the No. 4 copper loads crippled three times as many mallard as did the No. 4 lead. The No. 4 steel crippled four times as many, and the No. 6 steel crippled seven times as many ducks as did the No. 4 lead. In addition, the No. 6 steel shot was comparable in killing efficiency to No. 4 lead at 30 yards but lost much of that efficiency beyond 30 yards and continued to cripple mallard through 80 yards.

Copper shot proved more efficient in some tests; however, a study by the Illinois Natural History Survey showed copper poisoning to be just as deadly as lead poisoning, although it takes much longer to appear. Lead-poisoned waterfowl usually die within twenty-one days of ingesting lead pellets.

Another test called for the firing of 5,000 rounds of each type of shot through high-quality test barrels. After 5,000 rounds of steel had been fired, bulges of .0057 inch to .0065 inch were visible on the outside of the two test barrels at the chokes. Nearly half of the barrel deformation took place during the first 500 rounds.

Much of this deformation is merely cosmetic in nature and, according to Winchester, in no way affects the performance of the shotgun. And considering the normal useful life of a duck or goose gun (a 5,000-round limit would take the gun through many, many hunting seasons), the use of steel shot would not shorten the life of the average waterfowl gun in use today. Excluded are thin-walled double-barrel shotguns that could be expected to show more intense wear.

At this writing (late 1977), the Atlantic and Mississippi Flyways contain specified "hotspots" where steel-shot-only is the rule for waterfowl hunting. The hotspots were determined by the Field and Wildlife Service and various state fish and game departments and although the concept of hotspot restrictions has been fought (a case in point being an unsuccessful suit by the National Rifle Association), the plan remains and will be expanded in future seasons.

So we appear to be stuck with steel shot, at least around some of this country's more popular shooting wetlands. What does that mean to you and me?

It means relearning the capabilities of your duck gun. Steel shot loses its killing efficiency sooner than lead, offers a shorter shot string, and cripples more birds beyond 30 to 35 yards. Where No. 6 lead shot has been the choice in the past, we will now have to use No. 4 steel to gain about the same killing power. And sky-busting goose hunters, never a very successful group of hunters, will have to curtail their downrange firepower even more because Canadas, snows, and blues are big, heavy birds with heavy bones requiring more penetration than today's steel loads can provide, at least at marginal ranges. So we have some relearning to do.

Waterfowl Identification

If you can't identify ducks before you shoot, you shouldn't be shooting in the first place.

That is the best reason to bone up on what various duck species look

A greenhead (drake mallard) passes some blocks for an initial look-see. Mallard are easily the most popular sporting duck on the continent. (Photo courtesy Stephen Maslowski)

like in flight and on the water. Knowing your target keeps you from going over the maximum number of points as set out by the federal government each year; it also offers a sense of accomplishment and indicates that the hunter respects the game and the sport.

North America's most popular duck species can be divided into two distinct groupings, puddle ducks and diving ducks. Puddlers, sometimes called dabblers or pond ducks, are usually found in and around shallow wetlands, marshes, ponds, and lakeshores, while the divers are more at home on larger, deeper impoundments. Dabblers have legs positioned near the center of the body, tip up to feed, swim with the tail held clear of the water, and carry unlobed hind toes. Puddlers also spring vertically off the water on takeoff, rather than sprinting along the surface.

The most common and most popular puddler is the mallard (*Anas platyrhynchos*), which weighs about 2½ pounds and nests from the British Columbia coast eastward into Quebec and south to Colorado and the Midwest. The drake's head is a glossy dark green with an orange bill, and the hen is mottled brown. Both sexes have metallic blue wing patches.

The mallard eats both aquatic vegetation and field grains, and this should point the hunter to proper shooting locations.

One crisp September evening another hunter and I crouched in a weedy strip along the lure crop field in Manitoba's Carrot River Valley. It was an evening when the scarlet sunset seemed to last forever and we soon forgot about shooting and leaned back to watch the thousands of mallard, pins, and blacks form unending clouds of birds as they arose from a nearby slough. Cloud after cloud of big ducks filled the red sky

The pintail drake, a large duck, sports a jaunty tail spike and can fly at speeds approaching 50 miles per hour in a tail wind. (Photo courtesy U.S. Fish and Wildlife Service)

and I decided it was the most ducks I had ever seen on the wing at any one time.

Many of these birds were mallard that talked to one another contentedly as they settled into the lure crop and began eating the plentiful corn and oats. By the time we left an hour later the night was full of duck sounds; there must have been 20,000 birds within 200 yards of our location.

The pintail (*Anas acuta*) is a popular bird in the Far West, although its breeding range runs from the Pacific Coast eastward to Hudson Bay, favoring open meadows as nesting locations.

The drake pintail is a handsome and somewhat gaudily built duck, having a long, thin tail and an equally long neck. Both sexes carry a stripe on the rear edge of each wing, and the drake has a white stripe on the underside of the neck. Both male and female have a gray bill, but the drake's head is dark brown while the female's head is much lighter in color. The pin weighs in at about 2 pounds.

Pondweed, moist vegetation, and field grasses are the pintail's diet, although the bird willingly foregoes natural food for cultivated grain where available.

The black duck (*Anas rubripes*) isn't truly black. Both sexes are colored a dusky brown except for immature birds that show white under-wings and a lightly striped breast. The adult drake's bill is almost always more brightly colored than the hen's, having a greenish-yellow or pale orange bill; the hen's bill shows a good deal of black spotting, particu-larly near the base. Both sexes have a vague dark stripe running hori-zontally across the head that intercepts the eye.

Found mainly in the eastern half of North America, the black nests from eastern Manitoba to Newfoundland and south into a few eastern states, usually in wooded areas or dense fields featuring clumps of trees.

Some crossbreeding has been noted between blacks and mallard, especially in the eastern section of the black's range. Perhaps this is the reason the black's numbers have been decreasing in recent years.

The wood duck (*Aix sponsa*) drake is probably the most brightly colored common duck. Its head bears a jaunty crest and the entire head is colored green, bronze, and blue with a white throat and chin. The little woodie (average weight about 1½ pounds) favors tree hollows for its

The drake wood duck is perhaps the most brightly colored duck in North America. It is found along rivers and small streams. (Photo courtesy Karl H. Maslowski)

Woodies nest in tree hollows along river-
banks and in flooded woodlands. This
hen seems delighted with her home,
even if the entrance may be a little snug.
(Photo courtesy Karl H. Maslowski)

nesting, especially hollows found along wooded streams and in drowned woodlands. The bird takes well to artificial nesting boxes placed along stream and lakeshores; be sure to install a predator ring around the post between water and nesting box.

Since much woodie hunting is done along small rivers and streams, putting a dull-colored canoe on a small waterway is a perfect way to jump-shoot the species. A method I like puts one man ashore well upstream from known wood duck resting and feeding areas, while his partner remains in the canoe. The shore hunter moves back from the water and circles below the hotspot while his partner floats quietly downstream. In this manner the floating hunter gets one or more shots when the woodies flush before him from the water, and his partner gets some pass shooting as the birds flee downstream, usually along the path of the river. The little ducks often turn around in flight and fly back to their starting spot, giving both hunters another shot or two. Woodies are, as of this writing, 90-point ducks, however, so two would be the day's limit under a 100-point system.

It's sometimes tough to distinguish one duck from another, especially when one of the birds is a hen. A fellow outdoor writer who shall go unnamed was hunting blue-winged teal not long ago when a brownish-dark bird slid over the trees and flew within range. The unfortunate chap touched off his 12-bore and the duck crumpled. Before he could retrieve it a game protector stepped from behind a tree and identified the duck

Bluewings are the most numerous teal and make up the bulk of the nation's teal harvest each fall. They are fast flyers and travel in flocks. (Photo courtesy Karl H. Maslowski)

as a hen woodie and not a teal. The incident cost the hunter $30 in fines and no end of embarrassment when it hit the local hotline.

The woodie is a vegetarian, preferring nuts, acorns, seeds, and a few aquatic plants. Once near extinction, the wood duck has made a remarkable comeback and today is behind only the mallard in annual bag checks in the Mississippi Flyway.

Few waterfowlers would fail to identify the shoveler's wide bill and meshlike feeding filters. (Photo courtesy Karl H. Maslowski)

The American widgeon nests along the Canadian arctic coastline and provides some locally important gunning. (Photo courtesy Karl H. Maslowski)

The teals (*Anas spp.*), of which there are three species on this continent, are small, fast-flying ducks with characteristically fast wingbeats. All are most often seen in flights of from six to fifteen birds, rather than alone.

The blue-winged teal (*Anas discors*) is the most common teal; the drake is darkly colored and has a white crescent stripe in front of its eye. The hen is a darker brown in color. Both sexes have a chalky blue wing patch from which the teal gets its name.

The green-winged teal (*Anas crecca*) also has a dark body but is a bit gaudier than its bluewing cousin because the drake has a dark tear-shaped patch around each eye and a vertical white bar across each shoulder. Both sexes have a white belly and a green, metallic speculum (wing patch).

The cinnamon teal (*Anas cyanoptera*) is the least common of the three species and is completely protected in some Midwestern states. Like the bluewing and greenwing, the cinnamon averages about 12 ounces total body weight and is a fast flyer.

The shoveler (*Anas clypeata*) gets its unlovely name from its distinctive bill, which is long and unusually wide. Ugly or not, however, the appendage serves well when the duck feeds along muck bottoms for bits of animal matter, which it eats along with vegetable matter. Because of its mixed diet, the shoveler isn't considered as good on the table as the !lard, pintail, and other big ducks.

The canvasback is considered endangered and carries a 100-point value. Its numbers are seriously reduced over nearly all of its range. (Photo courtesy Karl H. Maslowski)

The drake has a bright green head, and both sexes have an equally bright blue shoulder patch. The drake has chestnut-colored sides and a white chest, while the hen is dull brown.

It isn't likely that an experienced waterfowler would take a shoveler from his retriever's jaws and not be able to identify it—the bird's wide, sloping bill is too distinctive—but for those who might be new to the sport, here's a surefire way to tell if that bird is in fact a shoveler. Check at the rear of the bird's mouth, where the bill meets the head. If this area contains tiny meshlike structures, the bird is a shoveler. The bird uses these to sift food from marsh sediment.

The American widgeon (*Mareca americana*), also called the baldpate, is easily identified by its white crown and its metallic green and black speculum. The male's head carries an equally bright green eye mask and distinctive white shoulder patches. The baldpate nests on dry ground in grassy depressions and beneath small shrubs and bushes. It ranges from the Alaskan-Yukon border southeast into the northwestern United States and in lesser numbers across the top of the Canadian mainland to New Brunswick.

The canvasback (*Aythya valisineria*) is a large diving duck distinguished by a wedge-shaped head and bill that is usually easily identified in flight. The male has a dark chestnut-colored head, a black chest and a white body, while the female is a dull brown with a gray back. Both sexes have dark brown wings with gray patches. The can nests most often on reed beds found over water although some individuals nest on dry land.

Continental populations of the can have become so reduced in recent years that the bird has become a 100-point duck. This means the hunter who is unwise enough to shoot the can has completely filled his daily point limit on ducks and must (if the law is to be obeyed) stop shooting. Unfortunately, too many duck hunters take advantage of most states' interpretation of the law to knock off the endangered can when ducks of lesser point values have already been bagged. Say, for example, the hunter had already collected 90 points worth of ducks when a canvasback slid past his blocks. The hunter bangs away with his shotgun and the duck falls and is bagged. Most states consider the hunter to be technically legal because his last bird reached or surpassed the maximum 100-point daily limit, yet the hunter's *total* daily point accumulation was actually 190 points because the last bird he shot was worth 100 points.

The can also has been hung with the term of "mistake duck," meaning it can be shot during those pre-dawn minutes when positive duck identification is virtually impossible. Here again the unscrupulous gunner can bang away with relative impunity from the letter of the law, and the canvasback is the ultimate loser.

Another large and endangered duck with coloration similar to that of

The redhead is also a high-point duck. It is a fast flier and is colored similarly to the canvasback. (Photo courtesy Karl H. Maslowski)

the canvasback is the redhead (*Aythya americana*). The redhead has a pronounced high forehead and the male carries a rust-red head and neck, a black chest, white breast, and a dark gray body. The female has a white breast and a brownish body. Nests are built either on reed tufts or on dry land.

An increasingly important and destructive predator of the eggs of both redhead and canvasback is the raccoon. This masked marauder, no stranger to water or marsh, invades waterfowl nests in search of duck eggs and even ducklings, and there have been cases in the South where man-made impoundments have flooded woodlands and marsh, making the nests of waterfowl located there more vulnerable to the nightly raids of raccoons.

The lesser scaup (*Aythya affinis*) is a jaunty little duck that nests over much of western Canada and is a locally important diver. The male sports a glossy black head with purple sheen, a black chest, pale gray body finely barred with black. The female has a light brown breast and has a white area behind the beak.

The ruddy duck (*Oxyura jamaicensis*), a small diver, has a fanlike tail of stiff, pointed feathers that is carried erect while swimming. The male has white chin coloration, a black skull cap, and a chestnut-toned body. The wings are dark gray. The hen is mottled brown in color and

A pair of Canadas streak over a flooded woodland before settling down to eat and rest. These big birds are among the toughest to kill of all waterfowl. (Photo courtesy U.S. Fish and Wildlife Service)

has a brownish horizontal stripe dividing her white cheek patch. The ruddy nests mainly through northern Alberta and into the British Columbia interior.

Old-squaws (*Clangula hyemalis*) are diving sea ducks found along both coasts. They sport feathers unlike any other maritime waterfowl. The male has distinct summer plumage of bold white and dark brown patterns, while its winter coat features an oval eye patch of dark brown, starkly white neck and chest, and a harness-shaped brown barring around the lower chest that fades down the back into a brownish tail. The tail is unique in its long, pointed central feathers that resemble those of the pintail.

The old-squaw breeds along the arctic coastline and on the arctic islands, building its nest right on the tundra's dwarf vegetation.

The Canada goose (*Branta canadensis*) has probably caused more waterfowlers to choke up than all other gamebirds combined. The bird's size alone is enough to make a grown man blow holes in thin air while the goose sails past at long range with the wind in its tail. Add to this the fact that the majority of successful shots taken at these big birds fall between the 50- and 65-yard range, and all-too-frequent misses are more easily understood.

There are several races of Canadas, but all are distinguishable by a wide chin strap of white and a white bar found between rump and tail, and the back and scapulars are black or brownish-gray. The belly is tan or light brown and the chest is a pale gray, while the wings are a soft brown with pale linings.

Mature honkers usually mate for life and are virtually inseparable, especially in nesting season. Fierce defenders of their offspring, adult honkers have been known to drive foxes, cats, dogs, and even men from their nest sites, hissing loudly, lowering their menacing heads and beaks to ground level, and beating their muscular wings against the ground.

Once hatched, goslings are light yellow for several weeks and follow their parents attentively. As the young birds grow, they appear almost identical to their parents, if somewhat smaller. This is the season when several state wildlife agencies choose to capture the young birds long enough to place bands on their legs. The bands bear coded numbers that will later determine how far the bird has traveled, its age, and its migration route.

Many artificial nesting boxes are used on state areas used by paired Canada geese. This Ohio officer makes sure the box and contents are suitable.

The lesser snow goose, handsome in its white, blue, and black plumage, is second only to the Canada in numbers. (Photo courtesy U.S. Fish and Wildlife Service)

But if young Canadas can't fly, they certainly can run. Picture a dozen or more grown men chasing wildly honking young geese; the birds sprint and dodge while the wildlife officers feint, dodge, and fall all over themselves in an attempt to grab a foot, a wing, even a neck, long enough to clamp a light metal band in place. This is no game for the man out of condition, for the geese never give up easily and never seem to run out of breath.

Races of Canadas differ in overall size and weight by a considerable margin. Interior races may weigh only 7 to 12 pounds and sport wing-spans up to about 6 feet, while the greater Canada has wings stretch-ing nearly 7 feet and a body weight of up to 20 or more pounds.

Not long ago I was aboard a small commercial plane flying a few thousand feet above the Rocky Mountains between Eagle and Denver, Colorado, when a passenger across the aisle pointed out his window and said we must be going to have an early winter. I took a look and there, a few thousand feet below the plane, flew a hundred or so white birds totally unruffled by the passing of our flight. They were lesser snow geese, most numerous of American geese after the Canadas. Flying in a loosely knit flock, the snows' white bodies and black wingtips were easily distinguishable against the dark green spruce and pinewoods of the Colorado mountains. As lovely as their name, the birds pressed south-ward, even though it was only mid-September and chill had not yet be-come permanent. They flew at more than 50 miles per hour.

Snow geese, for all their beauty in flight, can be rather easily decoyed. Hunters draped in white sheets and bits of white rags or pillow cases scattered about a known feeding area draw the handsome white birds to waiting guns and standing hunters. Grainfields are favored shooting spots, once the snows establish regular feeding routines.

The lesser snow weighs between 4 and 6 pounds. Its body is an overall white with rusty coloration on the head and breast. The wing primaries are coal black and the feet are red. Young snows are a uniform gray color. The so-called blue goose is actually just a color phase of the lesser snow. It travels in broken lines when alone or mixes with other geese when they travel the same route. The blue's body color is a blue-gray and the head and neck pure white.

The Ducks Unlimited Story

When the severe drought of the early Thirties threatened to dry up most of western Canada, it was discovered that up to 75 percent of all American waterfowl depended upon wetlands in this region for nesting area. An organization calling itself More Game Birds in America did some research and found that existing lakes, rivers, and ponds in the target area of Canada were insufficient to assure a large and continuous supply of waterfowl. Some seasons were too dry, others were too wet, and it became clear that extensive work needed to be done if waterfowl were to remain plentiful.

Federal law in both Canada and the United States prevented the spend-ing of public tax dollars for the project. This led to the formation of a privately funded organization large enough to keep the all-important nesting area in water.

On January 29, 1937, Ducks Unlimited, Inc. was founded and the drive for working funds was begun. A year later, Ducks Unlimited (Canada) was formed, and that same year Big Grass Marsh, D.U.'s first "duck factory," was completed in south-central Manitoba.

Since that rather modest beginning over four decades ago, D.U. has invested many millions of private dollars in over 1,000 water projects all over the Canadian Prairie Provinces. The projects range from huge Tom Lamb Wildlife Management Area near The Pas, Manitoba, to uncounted flooded potholes all over the middle west of Canada. I am certain that all those thousands of ducks a companion and I enjoyed seeing along the Carrot River Valley of Manitoba were there because of D.U.'s foresight and funding so many years ago.

At last count, some 251 species of birds, 60 different mammals and 10 species of fish use D.U.-created wetlands as home habitat, even though the many projects' target species were and are ducks and geese.

Critics of D.U. claim that the organization's generosity stems from a desire to raise waterfowl so they can be shot. To this D.U. responds: Were it not for the projects, there would be no ducks or geese at all. Here are the addresses where D.U. headquarters in Canada and the United States may be contacted:

Ducks Unlimited, Inc., National Headquarters, P.O. Box 66300, Chicago, Illinois, 60666.

Ducks Unlimited (Canada), 1495 Pembina Highway, Winnipeg, Manitoba, R3T 2E2.

Chapter 6

THE RIGHT DOG

"The *right* dog? Well, I hadn't really thought about it. I was just going to buy a dog to hunt birds with."

Unfortunately, far too many prospective dog owners approach this important decision with just this attitude. All too often the person buying a dog doesn't know much about any one breed and has probably hunted over fewer than four breeds in his entire life, which further restricts his thinking when it comes to choosing a hunting dog. The fact is, a good deal of thought and research should go into the decision because, unless the dog is sold or stolen, you will have to live with your decision for years to come, so you should make the best possible choice in the beginning.

So what is the best hunting dog for you? We could take a tip here from a fisherman in need of a new rod and reel. He first decides what gamefish he will fish for, then buys an outfit designed to go after that fish species. It's the same with a new dog owner. Start by deciding what you want to hunt, and go from there.

There are nearly as many different hunting dog breeds available as there are game species to hunt. Since World War II, in particular, the so-called Continental breeds have been imported, greatly broadening the possible choices. Pointers, setters, and spaniels, to name a few, have become among this country's most popular hunting companions.

Even more basic than deciding on a breed is the hunter himself. That means you. What kind of chap are you? Short-tempered? Patient? Goal-oriented? Wishy-washy or assertive? Know what type of person you are before deciding on a hunting breed, or even whether to buy a young pup or a fully trained adult dog.

How much time do you have to devote to developing rapport with your

Bird dogs that are used in warm weather
need plenty of drinking water if they are
to remain in top running condition.

new dog? Will you build a backyard kennel, chain it to a doghouse, or give it the run of the house? The wishes of other members of the family must be considered, especially on those days when you're not around and the dog needs to be exercised and fed. And kennels have a way of filling up with feces rather quickly unless a cleanup regimen is the rule; would cleaning smelly dog droppings be beneath you? Remember, it's your dog, not your wife's, son's, or daughter's.

If you are a fairly patient person who knows what he wants and how to get it, chances are, given enough time, you could bring a pup along from initial yard training to doing as good a job over wild birds as you are willing to settle for. This presumes, however, that you will have enough free time and inclination to do the job. If not, by all means admit it to yourself before buying the dog; you'll both be a lot happier in the future.

A friend of mine has the kind of job that keeps him busy fifty hours a week at the office, plus another fifteen hours or so on weekends and evenings pouring over reports and such. He owns a pair of bird dogs of very fine stock, but because of his other responsibilities he has little time to train and exercise them. The results are not good. Neither dog performs well in the bird field or harkens to his commands. His bitch, which had been bred twice to field-champion stud dogs, was in poor shape because of too little exercise and pups were lost each time because of it. The last I heard my friend was determined to sell or give his dogs away and buy a new pup to start over. I wish him well, but hold no great hopes for better results the second time around.

Time is all important, not only for the basic yard and field training, but for building the rapport I am so convinced is necessary between a hunter and his dog. Rapport is getting along, being friends, liking each other, depending upon each other without great disappointment. It is you and your dog hunting together instead of the labor-management arrangement seen all too often when the hunter expects his dog to be little more than a hunting machine.

For the hunter, rapport can be as simple as liking your dog and showing it. Use reprimands that are matched to the infraction and with an eye toward the personality of the dog because some breeds take reprimanding better than others. For the dog, rapport means it should hunt happily for you, responding to commands and hunting to the gun because it knows such behavior will result in finding birds, getting to carry them in its jaws on the retrieve, and getting an approving pat on the head now and then. Perhaps most important from the dog's point of view, it is hunt with you or not hunt at all. Make this clear from the beginning and you'll be well on the way to developing a willing companion. This is as true for hounds as it is for pointing and flushing breeds.

Whether you obtain a new puppy or a started adult dog depends on your own time and effort. It's impossible to develop a fully trained hunt-

Hey Mom, I think I got left out!

ing dog of any breed if no one spends time with it. That someone is you unless you opt to spend the extra money (sometimes several hundred to a thousand dollars) for the services of a professional trainer. The results you can expect from that investment is a field-ready dog that should do a credible job of hunting according to the abilities of its breed.

I have sold many litters of pups, both hounds and bird dogs, and I am constantly amazed at the way some hunters go about choosing the particular pup they end up taking home. Some buyers ask no questions about either the sire or the bitch, depending entirely on visual determination of how a pup looks and acts. Some men bring their families along and seem to choose the pup that makes the biggest fuss over their children. Some buyers select the pup with a certain coloration and others choose the largest in the litter.

There is no surefire way of picking one ten-week-old pup out of a litter and knowing for certain that it is healthy, bold, wide ranging, and destined to be a top-notch hunter. Rather the puppy buyer must depend on first impressions and, perhaps most important, the puppy's potential, which is really all the breeder has to sell. By all means demand a certified copy of the pup's American Kennel Club (or other certifying agency) registration of breed. You should also receive a copy of the puppy's pedigree covering a minimum of five generations. Most reputable breeders supply some sort of certification from a vet that all pups have received initial shots, and most of the honest breeders will agree to take back any puppy that turns out to be ill or disabled within two weeks following purchase. This includes the unlikely evidence that the pup suffers from hip dysplasia, a crippling condition thought to be at least partially hereditary.

When I sell a litter, I record each buyer's name, address, and telephone number. I then call each buyer about a month after the sale to inquire about the pup's acclimation to new surroundings and its physical development. I believe this instills the buyer's trust in me as a dog breeder, and I have enjoyed relationships of several years' duration with some of my buyers who call whenever their pup wins another field trial or outshines other dogs on a quail hunt.

The first bird dog I ever owned, a Brittany spaniel bitch my daughters named Sally, pointed her first cock ringneck during a spring walk afield when she was five months old. I wanted to jump in the air and shout or maybe run to her side and make a lot of her achievement, but I held back and let her flush and chase the rooster until it disappeared and she came trotting back, pink tongue lolling and a smile on her face. On subsequent jaunts she found more and more birds, which caused her to gain independence and move farther and farther away in her ranging. Like most bird dogs, she paces herself when afield to match my pace, and we make a good team. She is not a great field dog by any means, but she does everything I have asked of her. And as long as the hunter is happy, why expect more from his dog?

Let's look at five representative bird dogs and try to match the right dog with the right hunter. It's not as tough as you might think.

English Pointer

If any bird dog personified the term class, it would have to be the pointer. Lithe, fast, flashy, and with a toenails-to-nose love of the hunt, the pointer has brushed aside the English setter as this nation's most popular (and field-trial winningest) hunting breed. The pointer is a big-running, ground-eating dog that usually cares little who its owner is as long as that person is a hunter. All else is secondary. It can be hard headed and therefore needful of a bit of rough handling until it decides you really are in charge. The pointer is thin-coated and therefore well suited to the warm climates of the American South and Southwest. Its short coat picks up relatively few burrs and thorns.

Although found in predominant colors ranging from all white to a very dark liver-blue combination, the pointer is usually mostly white with a

An honoring point. Pointing dogs should freeze into a point at the moment they detect that another dog has pointed birds. (Photo courtesy Dennis Gordon)

few large patches of liver and little ticking. Weight among males averages between 55 and 75 pounds and the shoulder height is about 2 feet. Bitches are smaller and more lightly built. Because of the pointer's relative indifference to human attention and affection, the breed makes only a marginal house dog.

The pointer's natural inclination to run fast and far makes it a better quail, field grouse, and partridge dog than a dog well suited for ruffed grouse and pheasant. It needs birds that will sit tight under a point, giving the hunter time to catch up with the bird and the dog.

English Setter

The English setter is often called the gentleman's dog because of its gentle temperament, relatively easy training adaptability, and its affec-

Down solid on birds, this English pointer's only flaw is the lowered position of its tail. Few hunters would quibble about such a minor flaw, however.

tionate personality. It is also one hell of a hunting dog. Although the setter is generally considered well adapted to hunting almost all gamebirds, the dog is particularly suited for the rough treatment of woodland and brush hunting for such forest birds as ruffed grouse and woodcock. It is a long-coated dog and this protects the skin from briers, thorns, and greenbriers.

The English setter, like the other breeds, can be found in almost any color combination of brindle, black, orange, liver, and white. Most setters I have seen wear a basic coat of white spotted and colored here and there with the darker shades. This tendency to basic white makes the English setter easy to see in dark, shaded woodland.

An English setter down solid on a bird is a handsome thing. Legs and full-length tail wear full feathering, a name given to the dense row of hair on the animal's undertail and the rear edge of each leg. On point, the setter looks like something out of a calendar painting.

A friend, who has owned and hunted generations of English setters, says he won't kennel a dog unless it is truly staunch (steady) on point. In fact, he says he wants his dogs to find and point birds so staunchly that the hunter should be able to go home for lunch, return, and find that dog still rigid in its duty. An exaggeration, of course, but the tale illustrates some people's devout attention to class and their refusal to settle for anything less.

Many recognized gun dog authorities keep and hunt Englishes, among them John R. Falk, manager of public relations for Winchester-Western and the author of two books on hunting dogs. At last report, John was kenneling, feeding, and hunting a half-dozen setters, and although he can speak with glowing words about many dog breeds, his eyes belie his

The English setter is a big rangy dog with the reputation of hunting large chunks of real estate at a full gallop. They are famous for their gentle temperament and class.

true affection when he speaks about his setters. Like any good dog man, John has no delusions about the best breed for his own days afield.

The English setter weighs from 35 to 55 pounds with the average in the upper 40s, although the full coat may make the dog appear even heavier. The eyes are bright and eager, the tail long and active, and the stamina good. I've hunted over an aged English setter owned by two friends. They also own a younger setter and run the two dogs together. The young animal is wide ranging and fast. She usually winds covey birds and is the first dog on point while the older setter makes do with an honoring point several yards to the rear. Once that covey has been flushed and broken into singles, however, the old dog comes into his own. The younger animal is just too energetic to slow down for single birds, leaving all the gravy for the older, slower kennelmate.

"We call Sam our singles dog. He never fails to find all the singles around and he can point each one without flushing others nearby," one of his owners told me. Setters, like wine, need a bit of mellowing although the average setter matures at about eighteen months of age.

I have known hunters who wished every bird-hunting breed found its birds as does the English setter. The breed runs with a high head, winding its birds from downwind and casting in a narrowing zigzag pattern until body scent locks the dog into its point. Some setters make excellent pheasant dogs, learning to slow and pin running birds, and some even learn to warily circle a nervous cockbird, perhaps fooling the pheasant into thinking there are two dogs instead of one.

Like any other dog species, the English setter clan has its dingbats. A blustery chap I once knew owned a three-year-old setter of angelic breeding that, claimed its owner, could hunt rings around any other bird dog he had ever fed a bone to. To prove it he joined me for an afternoon's ringneck hunting on a commercial hunting preserve. In four hours that wonderdog found no birds at all and spent most of its time with its nose in the grass rooting after field mice. The owner said his dog had a bad day. I think the man just had a bad dog.

If the size of the dog you choose is no great concern, the English setter makes a good family dog and can live in the house. The breed is gentle and affectionate and soon becomes one of the family. There are few more honest welcomes the working man can receive than the thumping of his setter's friendly tail on the carpet at the end of a long day in the shop or office. A pat on the head and a scratch behind the ears is all the dog requires—until the weekend and a day afield for birds, that is.

Brittany Spaniel

The Brittany spaniel, the only spaniel breed that points as well as retrieves its game, was originally a Continental breed developed in Spain,

France, and England. Some old-time Brittany breeders say the dog was a conglomeration of existing breeds crossbred to develop a close-working, responsive dog that barked little and was used to help peasants poach hares and grouse from private fiefs. This is unsubstantiated, however.

The Brit's popularity in this country really took off following World War II when the huge farms were broken up into smaller plots and families moved into the suburbs with their small fenced yards. A bird dog was needed that worked close to its hunter and therefore did well on small farms, and would adapt to cramped suburban quarters. The Brit filled both requirements nicely.

The bouncy, energetic little Brittany makes a family dog well suited to

Who couldn't love a face like this?
Spaniels and setters thrive on human
affection.

An overzealous Brittany spaniel jumps when the chukar it was pointing flushed. There's more training needed here.

either kennel or house life. A close and affectionate association with family members can be of value in developing a hard-working, eager-to-please Brittany. A dog that quickly learns to identify home and family as something special, the Brit makes an alert and protective watchdog around the place, although its barking would, I suspect, seldom be followed by a bite. The Brit is just too gentle for it.

I have owned Brits for some time. One bitch in particular does a steady job of reassuring my wife about home security whenever assignments take me out of town. When I am gone, she tells me, the bitch is alert to every small sound anywhere around the house, even those too faint for human ears. I really feel better about being away, knowing the dog is on guard duty back home.

The Brittany is not blessed with the classic style of the pointer or the

The Brittany spaniel's zest for the hunt makes up for its often unclassical pointing posture. This little Brit has pinned some bobwhite quail in a fencerow.

loftiness of the setter. Born tailless or made nearly so by a vet's docking shortly after birth, and prone to point its birds a bit awkwardly when compared to some other breeds, the Brit at work is a lovely thing more in approach than in appearance. Its nose is excellent and Brits put on the ground with other breeds have more than once insisted a bird was around when other dogs abandoned the cover, only to be embarrassed when game was flushed.

The Brit is a medium-size dog. The breed averages about 19 to 21 inches at the shoulder and weighs between 30 and 45 pounds, with 38 about average. The coat is long and either flat or curly, and the legs are fully feathered. The ears are fluffy and the corners of the mouth seldom are damp enough to attract dust or pollen. A healthy Brit would rather weave through cover than blast a path, and dogs in tall, dense cover do the "Brittany hop," a hopping, jumping motion that provides forward movement through the tall stuff and keeps the hunter in sight.

The Brit is generally a close-working dog, although some field trial Brits think nothing of dashing 200 yards in front of the gun and judge in search of game. The Brittany uses the wind to scent birds, moves up on the scent line in a weaving pattern, and locks down on birds when body scent is encountered. It can be trained to be steady to both wing and shot, and it does a credible job of retrieving although a large cock pheasant can be quite a mouthful for the smallish Brittany. The Brit can be used for retrieving waterfowl provided the swim is not too long or the ice too heavy.

The Brittany spaniel comes in two colorations. The basic color is white, and spots and ticking may be of dark orange or a pronounced and handsome liver color. The orange coloration is much more common; some breeders insist orange Brits outnumber liver dogs ten to one.

The Brit is affectionate and gentle and even more susceptible to over-discipline than the English setter. The breed cannot absorb much physical abuse and commands given in a loud, overbearing voice can make a good Brit become aloof. If you are good with small children, you'll probably do well training a Brittany. The breed requires firm repetition and patience above all else, and responds very well to a friendly rapport between dog and owner.

Because the Brit is a close-working dog, it does well on a wide variety of gamebirds including quail, pheasant, ruffed grouse, woodcock, and even in the dove fields as a retriever. Its thick coat enables the Brittany to withstand cold northern winters, although this coat attracts burrs and the dog should be checked for chafing burrs at intervals during hunts in cocklebur country.

German Shorthaired Pointer

The shorthair might be thought of as the bird hunter's beagle because of the breed's determination to find game. The way the shorthair goes about this delightful chore may not please purist dog men—it has a habit of carrying a "low head," meaning the nose is often an inch or two off the ground even when the dog is ranging ahead and to the side of the hunter, instead of high in the wind in the manner of a pointer or setter. As a gamegetter, however, the German shorthair is hard to beat. Throw into the bargain a frame large and heavy enough to handle thick cover, a coat short but thick enough for moderately cold weather, plus an amiable disposition, and you have a popular, close-working gun dog.

There are two distinct lines within the German shorthair. The original breeding, which was imported to this country about 1925, was a large-boned dog weighing up to 70 pounds. Since that time, a lighter, more streamlined shorthair has appeared and it is this breeding that is most often seen afield today. The smaller German's coat contains more white, which is easily seen among weeds and woodlands.

The German is a willing worker and remembers its lessons well. It can be a good performer provided the gunner is satisfied with a dog that seldom strays too far from the gun. For this reason it is a popular dog among commercial game preserve owners who kennel bird dogs for the use of their clients. Here, too, the German's slight inclination toward

All pointing and flushing breeds should stay well in front of the line of hunters, then remain staunch on point until the birds are flushed or the hunter releases the dog after shooting.

hardheadedness may come in handy because preserve customers seem to enjoy shouting at their dogs as much as they do hunting, but the German just goes about its business of finding, pointing, and retrieving birds in a methodical manner. Germans have a reputation of seldom failing to find crippled but running pheasant, probably because of keen scenting ability and a propensity for running in a head-down position.

A game protector I once knew dearly loved to hunt bobwhites and owned a shorthair that had been the runt of its litter. The dog was small and because of its size seemed to get into fights whenever it was put down with another dog. One snowy day we were hunting bobs in a dense woods with another dog, a fine English pointer, and suddenly we heard threatening growls from inside a blowdown of fallen trees. After a search we found the two dogs facing each other from 2 feet way, and in between the dogs hid a probably very confused quail. Obviously each dog had pointed the quail at the same moment from different directions and were arguing over the point. Finally the much larger pointer yielded the field and backed out of the tangle, leaving the smaller but more determined German to its find.

The shorthair is not the brush-busting hunting machine its cousin the English pointer is, but has a slower, more deliberate pace that seems to nearly match the speed at which upland hunters normally walk. Back home, the German thrives on family attention and seems to do best living indoors rather than outside in a kennel. Its short coat and stub tail make the German shorthair a good house dog.

Weimaraner

The Weimaraner, or "gray ghost" as it was once called, is thought to have originated early in nineteenth-century Germany as a descendant of the red Schweisshund and possibly the bloodhound. It was developed by the nobles to the Court of Weimar who were great sportsmen and hunters of a wide variety of game native to early Germany, including bear, wolf, big cats, and boar. Large, sleek, and strong, the Weimaraner in its early uses was a generalist that trailed and brought to bay large animals. It also did a credible job on waterfowl and upland hares and birds.

Weimar's nobles formed a Weimaraner Club, drew up strict rules for membership, and kept the number of dogs in Germany to a reported 1,500 animals. All puppies born to member dogs were required to meet tight standards of size, color, and conformation, and pups failing to meet these standards were either killed outright or refused entry in the breed's stud book. Anyone wishing to own a dog at the time was required to join the club, but only after the members had closely scrutinized the entrant's reputation as a sportsman.

In 1929, an American named Howard Knight gained membership in the German club and returned to Rhode Island with two pups. Knight founded the American Weimaraner Club in 1941, but it wasn't until two years later that the breed was officially recognized by the American Kennel Club. Knight tried to enforce the same strict club rules as the German counterpart, but word of this so-called miracle dog quickly spread, drawing people from all over insisting on owning this animal with the capability of hunting both large and small game. The rumors were false, of course, and the breed just as quickly lost much of its following. Today's Weimaraners are used almost exclusively as pointers and retrievers of upland birds. They are not nearly as popular as other bird dog breeds, but a few stalwarts hang onto the breed and it is popular in bench show competition.

Today's Weimaraner is a handsome beast indeed. It bears a uniformly silver-gray or gray short coat over a large, muscular, and sleek frame that shouts speed in the field. The head is rather long, the eyes are amber or blue-gray and intelligent, and the overall bearing is alert, proud yet friendly. Males average up to 70 pounds with bitches something under that weight. Males average 25 to 27 inches tall at the shoulder, the females some 2 inches shorter. The dog's tail is docked but usually carried at a proud angle.

Field-trained Weimaraners make pleasant companions and can be quite productive on even the fastest runners, including the fleet ringneck and the ever-wandering chukar partridge. Its all-gray coat can make the Weimaraner tough to see among the weeds and brambles, however. The Weimaraner is a friendly dog and thrives on the attention of family members. It would rather live indoors, and can be a chronic complainer if confined to outdoor quarters.

Flushing Breeds

For the hunter who prefers the drive and determination of a dog bent on sending that pheasant or quail into a fluttering rise, flushing dogs are the right choice. Let's look at several flushing breeds that are commonly seen afield during bird season.

English Springer Spaniel

If ever there was a self-winding dog, it has to be the English springer. The hunting or field trial springer seems to be everywhere at once, quartering back and forth, not tarrying at any clump or cover yet seeming to encompass it all in a jolly and determined effort to locate and flush birds, and all within reasonable shotgun range of the hunter.

A hunter seeing his first springer work bird scent would think that particular dog was unusual; surely no entire breed offers such vitality afield, such determination and natural retrieval ability, such a biddable nature. And yet, most field springers are like that, a fact that undoubtedly accounts for the springer's wide popularity among upland bird and waterfowl hunters.

The springer may be among the oldest of established hunting breeds, having been mentioned in a French hunting book as far back as the fourteenth century. The springer's great ability to flush game for waiting hunting falcons brought it acclaim even in those days.

Today's springers are of two types, field dogs and bench dogs. Bench springers weigh about 50 pounds on the average and appear to have heavier, more solid builds and large heads. Brushed and combed for competition, they are impressive animals. The field type, although wearing the same thick, long coat of protective hair, weighs between 35 and 50 pounds and is more lightly built overall. The head is more alert and shoulder height is between 18 and 22 inches. The dog's thick coat, colored a basic white with liver or black spots and ticking, bears up well through the heaviest burr-infested cover, but this same coat must be laboriously picked clean of trash by the hunter at day's end.

Perhaps the best springer I ever had the pleasure to hunt over was owned by Nilo Farms, a model training school and game preserve located near St. Louis. The game was planted chukar partridge, a bird that stays put until flushed and flies well once in the air. The springer, a spry little liver and white bitch, had played the game many times before and knew to keep an eye on the dog handler at all times. Not once did the handler speak to the dog and only once did he softly toot a small whistle carried between his lips, yet the springer never went beyond shotgun range, never backcast behind the hunters, and never failed to hup (sit) when a bird had been flushed. One partridge carried its shotload into a very dense honeysuckle tangle before dropping and I was sure the bird was lost, a shame since it had been the second half of a double. The bitch wasn't convinced of this, however, and bounced off into the tangle. Within a minute she came galloping back, hupped at the handler's feet, and delivered the dead chukar before resuming her measured casts before the gun. Never before or since have I seen a springer perform as well over live game.

It might be worthwhile for you, as a prospective dog owner, to attend one or more field trials before choosing your dog. Each handler or owner in attendance at a field trial has a great deal of experience with his particular breed and knows what it takes to develop a complete field dog. Puppies usually are expected to show little beside drive and enthusiasm

Still wet from his workout in wet weeds, Marilyn and Jack Watkins' English springer, Tac, is ready to dive back to work if the command is given. The springer is perhaps the most enthusiastic of the hunting breeds. (Photo courtesy Wally Nelson)

Repetition is the key to teaching lessons to any dog. This springer will learn to release its birds into the handler's hands. (Photo courtesy Wally Nelson)

in puppy trial stakes, while all-age gun dogs must do it all: locate and point or flush game, be steady to wing and shot, and retrieve crisply. Hound trials are just as informative and can be fun to watch. Beagles are run on live cottontails while judges mounted on horseback follow, watching how accurately the hounds work out checks (breaks) in the scent trail and so forth. Most trials for coon and fox hounds are laid with artificial means over an established route. Water trials for coon dogs involve a caged but unharmed raccoon drawn over a body of water on a small floating platform. The dogs swim along behind and the first dog to reach a predetermined point on the far shore is declared the winner.

The simple observation of any type of field trial probably wouldn't help in a decision about which breed or age of dog to buy, but talking to experienced dog people certainly will. All you need to do is tell someone at the trial that you are thinking about buying a dog and suddenly you'll have a knot of interested people around you, offering advice, explaining available lines of breeding, recalling litters of available pups, and perhaps downgrading dogs of competing breeds.

It's also a good idea to talk to one or more of the judges at field trials. They invariably have long experience in casting a critical eye at hundreds of talented hunting dogs and know exactly what to look for in a better than average entry. Tell the trial folks the uses you plan for the dog, how it will be kenneled, and a little about your own experience in training dogs. More than likely they will prove helpful in the selection process, even if to a man they usually are forever loyal to the dog breed of their choice, be it beagle or wirehaired pointer.

Not only does the springer please in the field, its friendly, affectionate temperament makes it an ideal house dog as well. It gets along easily with children.

Labrador Retriever

For the person who enjoys waterfowl and upland bird hunting with equal zest, there can be no better choice than the amiable black dog with the smiling face, the Labrador retriever. Whether used to retrieve fallen waterfowl, flush and retrieve upland birds, or both, the Lab has in recent decades gained an ever-growing number of fans who will not tolerate talk about other dogs being the Lab's equal. If you insist on such talk, do it with a Lab man who is smaller than yourself.

The name *Labrador retriever* is somewhat deceiving since the breed is thought to have originated in Newfoundland, not Labrador. It wasn't until the 1920s that considerable numbers of these dogs arrived in this country, and it was nearly a decade after that before a specialty club was formed. It has been one success after the other for the black breed since then.

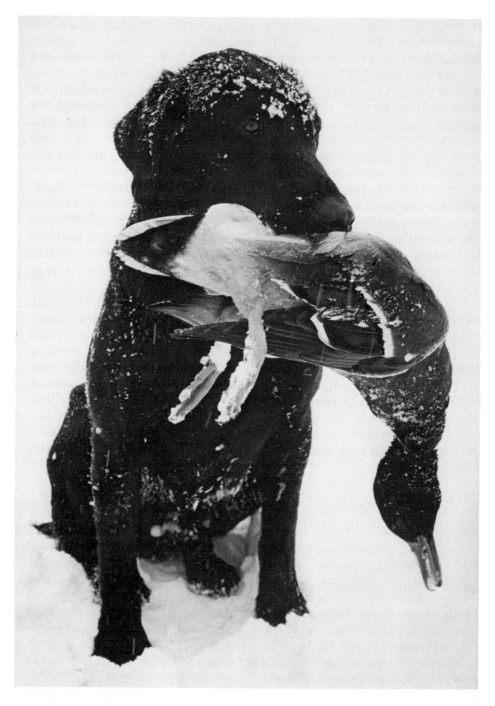

The Lab is undoubtedly America's most popular waterfowl retriever, and some double as upland flushing dogs.

The modern Lab is almost always completely black, although a few yellow and chocolate-brown Labs are seen. The dog's coat is relatively short and smooth and has a high oil content making the breed well suited to life in the water. A rather large dog, the Lab averages about 2 feet high at the withers and weighs between 60 and 75 pounds and has a rounded, full-length tail. The Lab's disposition is similar to that of the Brittany spaniel—eager to please, affectionate, and excellent around children. In fact, although the Lab can be kenneled outdoors if started there at a young age, it much prefers to be part of the family if the house is large enough to accommodate that much dog.

I have a friend who either owns two Labs or is owned by two Labs. Which is the case has not yet been determined, but I'm betting on the latter. The dogs have a first-class backyard kennel but, determination by my friend to the contrary, always seem to end up in the living room every evening the family is at home. Like many hunting breeds, the Lab can be a family pet one day, a hard-working field dog the next, so such favored treatment shouldn't ruin the dog's hunting ability.

The Lab, as might be expected, is an apt pupil with a willingness to learn. This is all to the good because most waterfowl and upland hunters demand much of their Labs. The dogs must be highly responsive to spoken and whistled commands, and be able to correctly interpret arm signals when a hidden duck or pheasant is to be located and brought to hand. Labs on waterfowl retrieval duty must sit quietly in the blind or skiff until birds hit the water, then await the command to fetch. They must be able to withstand icy water, sleet, and snow, and crippled ducks that won't cooperate by holding still in the water. They shouldn't stop or mouth the game unnecessarily during the retrieve, and a good Lab shouldn't argue with its handler over who gets the duck. There are many

Go! A willing Lab braves the chilly water to retrieve his master's kill. (Photo courtesy Michigan Tourist Council)

139

things for the Lab in training to learn, and most Labs learn them well.

The Lab is not quite the bouncy flusher as are spaniels, but it is fully capable of doing an acceptable job. Like the springer, the Lab should cast back and forth before the gun, always remaining within shotgun range. Upon scenting birds the dog should intensify its efforts to pinpoint the bird and rush it, forcing it into flight. If the bird is killed, the dog should mark its fall and make a crisp, no-nonsense retrieve on command, then continue casting for scent.

In the upland-field half of a Lab trial, the scented dummy is hidden a hundred yards or so from the dog and handler, and out of sight of the dog. At a word from the judge, the handler sends his dog along a desired route to the vicinity of the dummy, then works the dog with hand and arm signals while hoping to keep whistled signals at a minimum. In this way the dog is expected to locate the dummy by following the handler's directions, then make a quick retrieve. This type of training has obvious advantages when in a duck marsh and a bird has fallen well out of the dog's sight.

Golden Retriever

Far less popular in terms of field dogs in use but no less trainable than the Lab is the golden retriever, a long-coated dog of comparable size and amiable temperament. The golden's history in this country is a short one. The golden was not accepted for recognition by the American Kennel Club until 1932 and for another fifteen years or so the breed was a relative rarity in this country. Elsewhere, the golden's history is longer, with the English recognizing it in 1910 and the Canadians in 1927. Once that first noteworthy field championship was attained (in 1939, by a dog owned by Paul Bakewell III of St. Louis), the breed was on its way.

Excellent nose, temperament, and hunting instincts aside, the golden's good looks alone might have won its popularity. Most striking is the animal's handsome golden to light russet coat. The coat is long and luxurious and includes full feathering on the dog's legs, tail, and underbelly. Brushed and trimmed, the golden is an exceptionally handsome dog. But this same coat of dense, fine hair has a way of picking up burrs, thorns, weed seeds, and a variety of other trash during a day's hunt in cover, and the coat's color shading can, in some types of cover, make the dog tough to see against weeds of similar shade.

Like the Lab, the golden is probably most at home for the waterfowl hunter. Its dense undercoat and a longer outer layer make it nearly impervious to water and it has a strong instinct to locate and retrieve birds. The golden is eager to please and is very trainable. Like the Brittany, the golden is best coaxed into doing the right thing rather than forced into it. The breed cannot tolerate much rough handling and many owners claim this is because the dog is simply too heady, too smart, to be force-trained. It isn't likely the golden is any smarter than the Lab, yet the breed has a way of apparently knowing what is desired and doing it, even though the Lab may be mature at age eighteen months while the golden often requires twice that amount of time before optimum performance is reached.

The golden retriever would have to be classed as a big dog. Males average 23 to 24 inches high at the withers with bitches about an inch less all around. Males weigh between 65 and 75 pounds each; females about 5 pounds less. The ears are flat with rounded tips and are carried against the head; eyes are confident and eager.

I once spent an enjoyable morning hunting ringnecks with a friend who used a five-year-old male golden. The birds were plentiful and it was a great day just to be outdoors. But adding to this fine combination were the antics of Job, the golden retriever. His owner said he had named the dog Job because it took the patience of that biblical character to hunt over a dog that thought he could hide behind every blade of grass with the dead bird in his mouth. The handler, with the smile of a man who was amused rather than annoyed by the dog's antics, would say, "I see you, Job," and the dog would immediately trot over and deliver the pheasant to hand. It was a game that was repeated every time a retrieve was made, and neither of us minded a bit.

"I let him get away with this act early and now I guess I'm stuck with it," said the owner with a smile. "But if it hadn't been for the dog's antics, I couldn't have named him Job, could I?"

As someone who has on occasion permitted his own dogs to develop their own idiosyncrasies, then put up with them through the dogs' adult lives, I understood. I believe these traits personalize the relationship between man and dog—and the golden is a very personable dog.

Trailing Breeds

Perhaps trailing hounds are thought of in more romantic terms than are the pointing and flushing dogs because the trailers chase their game and maintain contact with it for an extended period. A good chase has long been dramatized in films and stories, so it is no surprise that hunting involving the chase would have a devoted following.

There are hounds that trail their quarry by scent and those that chase it by sight. Because the former type is much more commonly used by hunters in this country, we will deal exclusively with trailing hounds.

Beagles

For a number of years, the beagle was America's most popular breed of dog of all the hundreds of breeds available. Today other breeds have overtaken the beagle as the country's top dog, and perhaps this is for the best. The beagle is back where it belongs, among the dedicated rabbit hunters and field trialers who love a good chase and the music of a singing hound with a snootful of bunny scent.

Attend a beagle field trial and it will prove a real education. Unlike bird dog trials where many handlers refuse to use their dogs for hunting as well as trialing, the beagle trial is a gathering of men and women who love beagles first, rabbits second, and hunting a fast third. In fact it would be difficult to separate the three. A trial hound might be hunted a time or two through the week, then put down before a trial judge on the weekend—with the handler fully expecting his dog to excel at both tasks.

The beagle trial is a comfortable afternoon of easy talk between dog owners and judges, the choppy talk of a beagle brace after a rabbit, and the excited shouts of the men whose job it is to flush rabbits for the trialers. Experienced trial dogs have the system down pat. While leashed and awaiting their turn on the line, the trial dog does a little scratching, a little sniffing, a little whining to get closer to the next dog down the line. But once it is led out front and a rabbit is started, the little dog is suddenly all business. The mounted judge follows where he can watch for missed checks, backtrailing, and other faults and the gallery makes its own judgments as each brace is picked up following a chase.

The word *beagle* originated from the altered French word *beigle*, meaning small. The first beagles to see America were imported by General Richard Rowett of Carlinville, Ohio, in the 1870s. At about the same time two other gentlemen introduced beagles here, and the love affair began. In 1884, the English-American Beagle Club was formed and General Rowett was appointed to a committee to draft standards for the breed. What resulted was a dog that filled a wide gap among U.S. sportsmen—a dog small enough to be easily cared for, yet keen enough in nose and desire to hunt a solid eight hours before the gun.

Today two sizes of beagles are recognized. The larger of the two measures something over 13 inches high at the shoulder and is known as a 15-inch beagle, even though it may not reach quite that height at the withers. The smaller of the two sizes, known as a 13-inch beagle, includes any beagle measuring up to, but not surpassing, 13 inches at the shoulder. Some beagle club members and trial judges can be quite sticky about proper measurement and classification and make it a point to measure all dogs before running them in competition.

When it comes to rabbit hunting, some hounds are quite content to lay back in a brace of dogs, letting the other animal work out the checks. But there are a few beagles, known as strike or jump dogs among beaglers, that insist on running in front in all chases and seem to thrive on wiggling under every bit of cover in hopes of starting the rabbit from its form.

I once kenneled a pair of beagles that couldn't have been more un-

Beagle field trials have made the hills of America ring for decades. Even though these handlers look rather glum, they really are quite proud of their ribbon-winners.

alike. Jay, the younger, male dog, insisted on lining out fast on every trail the dogs ran. He was flashy with a deep, chesty bawl and so fast he sometimes missed checks where the rabbit had leapt aside and changed directions, and it was up to his bracemate to put him back on track. That was Missy, a dainty little lady no more than a foot high at the shoulder but blessed with incredible scenting ability and the patience to keep her mouth shut until she smelled fresh rabbit scent. Missy was also a great strike dog, and I suppose for every one rabbit Jay blundered into flight, Missy must have started a dozen. She would burrow nose-first into every tuft of grass and logpile, and sooner or later out would pop a cottontail and the race would begin.

Today trial judges tend to favor the super-fast field trial dogs, and I suppose that is all right for those who prefer to trial their dogs instead of hunting them. But I believe the hunter is better off with a more deliberate beagle whose slower pace puts fewer rabbits to ground under farm equipment and down groundhog holes.

If you are satisfied with stereotyped dog colorations, look at the beagles pictured in the encyclopedias. They usually have brown heads, lower sides, and tails; the belly, muzzle, and tail tip are white and the back is covered with a solid-black blanket, save perhaps for a single white patch on the hips or lower neck. But don't expect this typically colored beagle to represent all of the full-blooded beagles seen running rabbits for hunters or field trialers. Beagles of excellent lineage can be colored in every combination from nearly all white to solid brown—and everything in between. So-called black-blanket beagles are pretty to look at but hardly typical of the breed.

Coonhounds

It is a cool, damp night in late October and a harvest moon silvers the silhouetted woods and makes the shadows seem impossibly black. Three coon hunters leave darkened cars along a farm lane and pace off into the woods, their five-celled flashlights sending white fingers of light among the trees. Straining at five leashes is a pack of coonhounds—a black and tan, two redbones, and a bluetick; the fifth dog is a treeing Walker just learning the ropes.

When the party is well off the lane, the men pause long enough to slip the leashes off the dogs and the animals surge into the woods and are gone. One man strikes a sulphur match to fire his pipe; the blue smoke moves straight up in the still air.

It isn't five minutes later when the older redbone, a bitch in her fifth year, can be heard perhaps 100 yards away through the blackness. She is opening fast, her basso voice soon merged and blended with the voices of the other three mature dogs. Then the young Walker tries his pipes a bit tentatively and the entire pack is off on the far side of a wooded ridge. The men shake away their daydreams and plunge through the woods, dodging limbs, creekbanks, and brier patches. It takes them several minutes to close on the dogs, now baying treed in a grove of mature birch trees on a steep sidehill.

Puffing and stumbling, the three hunters reach the tree and stab the dark among its limbs with their flashlight beams. There, 30 feet above the ground in a thin crotch, rests the raccoon, its eyes showing yellow-white against the night. The younger man peers at the tree a moment, then grabs a low limb and begins climbing to the coon. The animal soon senses what is to come and moves higher in the tree, this time away from the main trunk on a flexible branch. The young man reaches the right level and begins shaking the limb. The coon slips underneath the branch, hangs there a moment, and falls to the ground. The hounds are on it immediately, each after a mouthful of coon and none caring which end it grabs. The young Walker tries to grab the large coon's neck and gets a slashed ear for his trouble. Then a redbone closes its trim jaws on the coon's neck and shakes it several times. The animal is limp now and the hounds worry the carcass until one of the hunters reaches in and lifts it out of reach.

The black and tan coonhound is said to have originated from the selective breeding of Virginia foxhounds bearing the desired coloration. This would almost assure today's black and tans of a goodly amount of bloodhound blood, and in fact the two breeds are somewhat similar in configuration and coloring, although the bloodhound is much fleshier around the jowls and eyes than its coonhunting cousin. The black and tan is a hardy animal, able to withstand the rigors of frequent chases and the chill and wet of winter. It is a particularly trainable, persistent hound and is blessed with a deep, authoritative voice that carries well through woods and fields.

The male black and tan averages up to 27 inches at the shoulder and weighs between 55 and 65 pounds. The breed's stamina is well known and its speed in the chase is accomplished with strong, well-proportioned running gear. The black and tan is a good treeing breed and can put a cagey old boar coon in a tree and keep him there until the hunter shows up to dispatch the coon or pull the dogs off.

The United Kennel Club recognizes six coonhound breeds: the black and tan, Walker, Plott, bluetick, redbone, and English, the latter also often used in foxhunting. Just because a good-running cooner has no registration papers or fancy pedigree is no reason to reject it as a fully capable coonhound. Many unregistered dogs of mixed breeding are used on coons in the United States, and they do first-rate jobs in the autumn woods. Your best bet in considering an unregistered cooner before purchase is to get into the swamps and fields with the dog on the first cool night and see what kind of job it does. Not only will this prove or disprove the owner's claims, it will also fill the night with the prettiest music since Gabriel blew his horn.

Chapter 7

TRACKS AND TRACKING

The big whitetail buck trotted out of the woods on my right, crossed a grassy ravine broadside to me, and disappeared in a thicket of honeysuckle. I was amazed that the animal was on his feet, much less running, because a hunting arrow was buried half its length in the near side of the deer's neck.

A few minutes later a camouflage-dressed bowhunter emerged where the buck had first appeared, scanning the surrounding woods, trying to locate his trophy. We walked to the point where I'd seen the deer enter the woods and I left him to look for spots of blood while I moved into the thicket to do the same thing.

We looked for no more than ten minutes when he called me over and said he was abandoning the search. I couldn't believe my ears.

"I know I hit him in the neck, but if he'd been hit hard we'd have found him by now," the man said, turning to go. "There are a lot of deer around here. I'm going back to my stand." And with that he shouldered his bow and strode off across the ravine.

I had to bite my tongue to keep from telling this man what I thought of someone who would arrow a fine trophy and then leave it to die, wasted, in the woods. I decided to find the deer myself.

Within five minutes I'd located the first dime-size drop of blood, still wet to the touch, on a leaf of honeysuckle. Soon a second drop was found, then a third, and I knew the direction the buck had traveled. The farther I went, the heavier the blood trail became until I topped out on a leaf-carpeted hardwoods hillside where the animal had paused long enough to shake the arrow out of his neck. The violent movement had covered a 10-square-foot area of ground with blood and I knew the deer, having lost so much blood, couldn't be far away.

Rabbit tracks through a woodlot often follow creeks that have frozen over. Such natural runways offer unobstructed travel and some protection from predators.

Less than 20 yards away, just beyond the woods in a small clearing, lay the buck. He had died in less than half an hour after being struck by the heavy hunting arrow, and he was in fact a trophy. His heavy antlers bore ten handsome points and looked to be symmetrical. I guessed the buck at about 200 pounds on the hoof, a prime game animal. The tracking job, once that first drop of blood had been located, was easy, so easy that blood alone had located the deer for me. Yet the bowhunter had given up this fine deer because he clearly didn't understand how to look for sign—and maybe because he was a little lazy.

A working understanding of how, why, when, and where game animals leave traces of their passing can add so much to a day afield. I get a kick if I happen to see the delicate round prints of a fox's passing while I hunt birds; in fact, the knowledge that fox tracks have appeared in a certain area can be stowed away for later use on fox hunts. Rabbit hunters should be happy to see fresh rabbit tracks in the cover they hunt, but knowing how fresh those tracks are, and which direction the animal was traveling, would help put that rabbit in the game bag.

Can you tell the difference between the track left by a hen pheasant and one left by a cockbird? If the tracks of a local elk herd show the animals to be moving along a ridge, would you know whether to make a stand uphill from the tracks, or downhill? And if you roll but don't kill a rabbit on a snowless day, could you find it by tracks and sign?

If your answer to this type of question is at best an honest *I don't know*, then maybe you'd better hone your woodsman's skills a little. They can help.

Tracks are left by animals that were, but are not now, standing in them. You can't eat tracks or sign, some guides have told me in an apparent effort to discount their importance; yet, if nothing else, tracks indicate the presence of game in your area. If the tracks are fresh, the game has been there recently; if they are old, they may have been made by an animal just passing through the area, or one using the route one time only. I'm encouraged when I find tracks, however old they may be. It is always better, it seems to me, than finding no tracks at all.

There are times, of course, when tracks alone are thin comfort indeed. I was hunting elk in the San Juans of southern Colorado a few years back and it seemed every square foot of ground was tracked up by elk. Shale slides, rock outcroppings, creeks, and meadows all bore the wide, cloven mark of elk feet, and the weather had been so dry for so long that determining their age seemed impossible. When we finally found elk it was because they marched out of an aspen thicket ahead of another hunting party, not because we were able to make use of their tracks.

Little of the Midwest can boast of ring-necked pheasant populations to match those of the 1940s and 1950s, and my home state of Ohio is no exception, so I am always pleased when I spot one or more sets of ringneck tracks along a field of picked corn, in a woodlot, or wherever. It means at least a few birds are about and it's just possible that some wary old rooster might make a mistake and meet my pointer sometime when I am loaded for birds. I most often see pheasant tracks alongside wire fencing bordering a grain field. It seems the birds use this as a travel route between the cover of the fencerow and the easy pickings of a grain field on the other side. Very often, if one set of four-toed pheasant tracks are partially blotted out by another, the cockbird is second in line while the hen leads the parade, not unlike a whitetail buck that sends

A deer left its track in hard-packed clay.
Such a track is almost impossible to age.

his does across a clearing first, then follows along if everything is safe.

Gamebird and rabbit tracks are usually found around food and cover because these animals seldom stray far from such spots. Big game, however, covers more territory and it's a wise hunter who knows where to look for tracks and sign, depending on the game he seeks and the terrain where he seeks it.

A western desert mule deer hunter should look for tracks around an area's one and only spring or watering hole since any local deer must go to the spot once a day to drink. The eastern deer hunter's choices are not so few; water is much more common in his country and local deer can find it in almost every bottom, valley, or basin. East or West, however, a good place to find tracks and other sign is always around water. Daylight and late evening are usually the best times to be there when the game is, although the hunter merely looking for sign can visit water almost anytime and expect to find signs left by his quarry.

As this is being written, I am making final plans for an elk bowhunt in a national wilderness area of the West within a few months. Since my hunting companions and I are here and the game is out there (in the West), we must rely on the guides employed by our outfitter to know where the herds can be found. To do this, at least one guide has already spent several weeks in the high country, looking for fresh elk tracks, droppings, and wallows, spotting good bulls through a scope, and generally keeping tabs on herd movements and condition. I know from personal experience how tough it can be to accurately follow individual animals over a dry mountain and I am thankful that the job lies with someone who has more experience than I. There will certainly be a good deal of hunting to be done to find trophy heads, but nothing like what would be required if we had to go into the mountains cold turkey.

These same hunting friends and I were after whitetails in the hilly woodlands of the lower Midwest one October day. We knew there were a lot of deer in the area and were looking for likely spots to erect tree stands. One mile-long, sloping ridge between deep valleys caught our eye and we spent a morning walking it. Within 200 yards of the road we began to find fresh deer sign; three buck scrapes were spaced perhaps 75 feet apart, and since all of them were about the same size, and the tracks in each seemed to match, we believed the same buck had made all of them. Farther down the ridge we jumped a pair of does from their midday beds in one valley so we stopped there to look for more sign. Sure enough, close examination of the thick carpet of dead leaves along the spine of the ridge showed the spot to be a regular crossing spot where the deer topped out en route from one valley to another. Half a mile away, where the ridge petered out in another valley, my partners found two exceptionally large buck scrapes within bowshot of a dilapidated old cabin with enough roof intact to make a safe stand. Within two weeks of the opening of bow season, all three of us had taken deer off the ridge stands. It is days of scouting like that one that convince me there is nothing so important in hunting big game than some intelligent scouting ahead of the season.

Of course, seeing all the sign in the world won't mean a thing if you can't—or won't—correctly interpret what you see. A compadre of mine wanted desperately to hunt a large southern farm that he was sure was loaded with deer. The farmer finally gave his consent but said he doubted the hunter would even see a deer. Two mornings later, following two sets of tracks along a ridge, the hunter shot a fine eight-point buck. He later related the story to the amazed farmer who then admitted he had seen plenty of tracks on his place but attributed them to his several dozen sheep that were given the run of the farm. The farmer couldn't tell the difference between sharp tracks left by a deer and those left by his sheep; it's no wonder he was amazed to discover his farm held deer.

I've seen this work the other way around and I'm still chuckling over the incident. I was still-hunting through an open woods for deer one afternoon when I met a young fellow coming the other way with his eyes on the ground and an earnest look on his face. Our brief conversation revealed he'd been tracking his animal for almost two hours and expected to get a shot any time. I wished him luck and we parted.

Thirty minutes later he returned along his backtrail. I hadn't heard a shot and asked if he'd jumped the animal he'd been tracking so intently. "Never did shoot at it," he admitted, his eyes on the toes of his boots. Pressed further, he drew a small circle with his toe, squirmed a little, and in a low voice admitted, "Well, when I came up on it, it was a pig." He'd been following some farmer's runaway pig for two hours thinking it was the biggest buck in the woods. This has happened to more than one hunter, but it's not the kind of story a man tells on himself around a campfire.

The successful use of tracks and other sign found in game country is really nothing more than keeping your eyes open and your mind working. Happening across a set of tracks means nothing if the finder doesn't associate them with the game he seeks. Ask yourself some questions. Are the tracks made by the game species you're after? How fresh do they appear to be? Was the animal standing, walking, or running when it left the prints? What was the animal's direction of travel?

If your game is deer it isn't likely you will confuse the tracks of other animals with those left by deer, although an exception might be the tracks left by desert sheep in country where whitetails or muleys abound. But there can be no mistaking the broad, cloven tracks left by moose or the dish-shaped prints of a caribou.

If the tracks are right, how fresh do they appear to be? Telling the freshness of tracks can save a lot of time by eliminating long, wearisome treks behind an animal that left its tracks a day, a week, or even a month before. I have seen tracks that appeared to be smoking hot, even though I had seen the animal leave them over a month before. Moist, shaded soil has a way of retaining tracks in surprisingly good condition for long periods, and dry arroyos of the West can shelter and protect tracks for amazingly long periods.

There are ways to tell the age of most tracks. Often weather can be a great help. If it frosted the night before and the tracks contain frost, it's a sure bet they were made before dawn—and probably well before. But if the area sustained a heavy rainfall the previous night and the tracks are still fresh and sharp even in a heavy rain, they have to be fresh.

Sometimes tracks can tell the whole story and make the hunter look helpless indeed. I was hunting deer in a big woods one December and our party walked out into the cover just at first light. On the way we passed a large buck scrape at least a yard wide, but since the hoof and tine marks were soft and obviously at least forty-eight hours old, we gave it no thought and went our way. We passed the scrape en route home that evening and found it to contain some impressively large tracks and antler marks from one edge to the other. The buck had been there to freshen his calling card since our morning visit, and it would have been easy to take a nearby tree stand and knock him off at close range. All we could do was swear under our breath and mentally kick ourselves a little.

A buck scrape is well named because the amorous buck uses it to tell the does in his area that he's the lothario of the deer clan and they could do no better than to submit to him. He conveys this message by using hooves and antlers to scrape out a patch of bare earth from 2 to 6 feet in diameter on the forest floor, usually directly under a low-hanging branch that he can hook and prod with his rack to get in the mood. Once the earth is prepared he spreads his hocks and splatters the earth with urine (and occasionally sperm) and mixes this smelly stuff with mud by scraping it with his tines and front feet. A large buck will make a large scrape and a small buck a modest one. Scrapes of all sizes are often made in series with one to half-a-dozen others along the buck's usual travel route, often a long ridgetop or creekbed. Their purpose is to attract does and advertise the buck's intentions during the fall rutting season, which in the North can vary from late September through December, and in the South from October through January.

The buck rub is created by the animal prodding and rubbing his antlers against vegetation, usually a small sapling, a woody bush, or some fallen branches. The rubbing urge begins in early fall when the thin, soft flesh covering the buck's newly developed antlers begins to dry up and peel; this itches and prompts the animal to remove it by scraping his antlers against trees and bushes. A new set of antlers is usually white or cream colored at the start but becomes stained as the rubbing continues.

About the time buck antlers are fully grown and the velvety flesh covering is removed, the mating (rutting) urge takes over. At this time the buck undergoes several changes; his neck swells up to twice its normal size and he forgets all about eating or sleeping. All he wants to do is fight and mate, fight and mate. If another buck isn't around to spar with, the buck vents his nervousness on nearby trees, often peeling away many pieces of bark and leaving the tree bleeding sap. A buck in this condition is as close to being a damned fool as any deer ever gets.

Find a fresh scrape or rub and you've found the home bailiwick of a rutting buck. I recall a handsome twelve-pointer I spotted across a wide clearing. When I first saw him the animal was facing directly away from me, but soon he turned broadside and just flailed the dickens out of a fallen tree at his feet. In fact, he was so intent on ripping that tree with his antlers that I was able to sneak across a completely open field and get within 30 yards before dropping him with a single shot in the neck. He never knew I was there.

The "tracking snow" sung in song and story is certainly of benefit, but only if the hunter knows what he's doing and can read sign. Wet, clinging snow has a way of making old tracks look new, particularly if there has been a hard freeze since the tracks were made. Powder snow is seldom much good for tracking unless you are dead certain the tracks are smoking hot because powder snow tends to make tracks soft and fuzzy. If the powder is very deep, of course, it makes the going tough for both the animal and the tracker.

I've known a few trackers who could seemingly follow a field mouse over hard granite and never miss a track; they had the ability to notice every out-of-place blade of grass and pebble and could tell you if the animal stopped to nibble on a leaf or detoured to check its backtrail.

A good deal of lore and mystery has sprung up around certain individuals because of their ability to stay behind an animal in tough circumstances. I am sure much of this mystery has been created by the city slicker hunter who is amazed at the thought of following animals by their tracks and sign. I once hunted with a fellow from New York who had never looked at a track in his life. He had shot a smallish deer and the animal had fallen down, gotten to its feet and moved off through a stand of cedars and over a low hill. He was sure he'd lost the deer, but I suggested we attempt to find the animal by sign. The blood sign was good, a drop or two every few feet, and we soon found where the deer had scrambled over some deadfall timber. Although the blood had lessened, I found a tuft of deer hair on the top of one log and a spot where the deer had fallen to its knees on leaving the deadfall. I sent him one way around the hill and I went the other, and within five minutes I heard him shout. The deer hadn't traveled more than 50 yards after falling and was already dead when we found him. The bullet had entered diagonally through the right side, clipped off the tip of one lung, and lodged behind the chest, and the deer had bled to death internally, which is why we found so little blood. To this day that fellow thinks I am a first cousin to Tarzan, only because we found a deer he'd given up for lost.

Even the best of trackers occasionally loses the trail and has to start over. One minute the sign is there and you're moving along at a good pace, then the sign has disappeared, vanished. Perhaps the animal has changed direction, perhaps the blood has stopped flowing, maybe the terrain has changed and tracks are no longer clear. The usual procedure in a case like this is to immediately return to the last good sign you found—be it track, blood or whatever—and start making larger and larger circles until more sign is found. It's a good idea to tie a handkerchief (red, not white) to a tree or bush where the last sign is located before circling. If the animal came this way—and that last sign said it did—you will probably cut its trail again by circling. Sometimes it is possible to figure the animal's direction of travel by drawing an imaginary line from the last sign to the one preceding it, but this is a shortcut and can sometimes send you off in the wrong direction.

I was bowhunting for whitetails one morning in Kentucky and had a standing shot at a fat doe no more than 30 yards away. My bowstring had no silencers at that time and when the string twanged the doe "jumped the string," leaping forward and taking the arrow through both hips instead of behind the shoulders. I saw the arrow leave her body and fly into a cedar tree 10 yards beyond. The doe jumped away and galloped down a wooded hillside into a brushy creek bottom. On retrieving the arrow I found it completely covered with blood and the spot where the doe had been bore a handful of arrow-clipped hair. But not one other bit of sign could I find—no blood, no tracks, nothing. A guide and I searched for two hours for that deer, finally abandoning the search when we decided the arrow had struck muscle and, although wounded, the deer would probably survive. The blood on the arrow had been bright red, indicating a muscle hit.

You can sometimes tell where your bullet or arrow has hit by the type of blood left by the animal. Bright, frothy blood indicates a hit in the lungs, which either collapses the lung immediately or fills it with blood and suffocates the animal. A lung hit is a good one and usually results in the animal being found within 150 yards, often stone dead. The lungs of most big-game animals are a large target compared to heart, spine, or liver, and certainly a top choice.

Bright, smooth blood indicates a hit in a muscle area and generally leaves little blood. Unless bullet damage is massive, muscle-hit animals will survive the encounter. Blood that is dark and sometimes speckled with bits of digested plants means a hit in the abdomen. A gut-shot deer will often lie down if the fright isn't too severe, then get up when the shock wears off to move away. If you don't get to gut-shot game right away it can mean a long and perhaps unsuccessful tracking job. The animal is in agony and will almost certainly eventually die, but it can travel quite a distance first and, once dead, the meat of an animal under such high stress can be hot and tainted.

There are animal signs other than blood and tracks that mark their passing just as surely, of course. All ground animals leave tracks, droppings, or dung. I have yet to see a game animal that goes out of its way to relieve itself; dung therefore is found where the animal feeds, near water, and along its daily travel routes. The size and age of the dung, and to an extent its content, can tell you a good deal about the animal.

Let's say you come across some deer droppings—teardrop-shaped, dark brown, and numbering from half-a-dozen to thirty pieces in a matter of a few feet. If the droppings are soft and pliable to the touch, they have been deposited within a few hours. If they are still warm to the touch, or steaming on a cold day, the animal is just ahead of you and probably not alerted to your presence.

With larger game animals than deer, the overall size of the droppings can help you judge how large their maker is. Great piles of droppings in one spot usually indicate a large animal that is at ease. A fresh track in a pile of droppings means at least two animals are traveling together because an animal almost never places a foot in its own dung.

An animal that has been shot will sometimes stumble and fall, leaving bits of hair on rocks, logs, and trailside trees. For example, a ram a friend of mine had wounded tried to cross a shale slide, lost its balance and slid halfway down the mountain in a shower of flying stone. We didn't have to look for the ram; the sound of the slide led us right to him.

If you're tenacious, you might want to try a solo type of hunting that calls for a thorough working knowledge of deer habits and following tracks and sign. What you do is single out a particular animal that is likely a trophy animal, because of the size of its tracks and their configuration, and you follow it carefully until the animal is spotted.

I like to hunt this way by myself although two men can do the job, one on either side of the tracks. You should remain off to one side of the trail as much as possible when tracking single animals, just in case the game loops back to check its backtrail or test the wind for scent. If you are tenacious enough to stay on its trail, chances are you will eventually get a glimpse of the animal ahead as it moves from one cover to another, lies in its daybed or feeds. This can be an all-day affair covering a lot of country, so take a sandwich and a compass.

There is at least one case on record when a deer tracked a hunter. A bowhunter in a tree stand idly watched a little spikehorn buck wandering toward the stand. The buck had his nose on the ground and it dawned on the hunter that the buck was following the trail of human scent right to the tree where the hunter waited. The hunter didn't want such a small deer and decided to have some fun with his curious visitor. When the spike got within 5 feet of the tree the archer stuck an arrow in the ground in front of the deer's nose. The little buck jumped aside, then reached out his nose and sniffed the shaft. Still not totally spooked, he moved right to the tree and followed the track up as far as he could reach. When the man and deer were eyeball-to-eyeball the man shouted "Get outta here!" He later reported the buck's eyes got twice their normal size and the animal almost turned himself inside out swapping ends and streaking away.

There are times, on big, dangerous game in Africa, for example, when following up wounded animals is mandatory, if not because of the hunter's willingness, then because his professional hunter's license requires it. But even when it's not mandated by law, even when the hunt is on your own private land, you should make every possible effort to track and locate wounded animals.

Chapter 8

BOWHUNTING

Infatuation with bows and arrows usually begins early, about the time a youngster is old enough to discover that playing in the woods is fun. The first bow is usually a homemade affair of rough-trimmed willow, while arrows are straight-stalked weeds or a few cheap arrows of wood purchased from a local hardware store. When I was a youngster two brothers and I formed a small archery club. The only way to gain membership was to collect a bird with a bow. Starlings were the easiest to knock off because they fed on the ground a lot and our frequent misses meant we usually located lost arrows burrowed under the grass instead of in the treetops. As our tackle improved along with our aim, we graduated to squirrels, raccoons, and the odd opossum unlucky enough to waddle out in the open. And there was a certain old milk cow that showed up at the barn one evening bearing two near-harmless arrows in her shoulder hump. The farmer never did discover who arrowed the cow, and we certainly didn't tell him.

Conversations with dozens of lifelong bowhunters convince me they have it all over gun hunters in the dedication department. In fact, many I have talked with have hung up their irons forever in deference to the bow. "After hunting with a bow for several years I just wouldn't be happy using a shotgun or rifle again," is the way they explain the changeover.

There are several standard reasons given, of course. A major one insists that bowhunting, because of the weapon's far shorter effective range, requires the hunter to stalk much closer to his quarry, and therefore be a better woodsman. He (or she, for that matter) must be more familiar with his quarry's habitat, lifestyle, natural wariness, and physical abilities. An arrow, unlike some of the slow, heavy rifle and shotgun slugs, cannot penetrate dense brush, so shot selection must be more precise. And personal satisfaction is a big part of it. Many hunters have said they never feel prouder than when standing over a deer or a cottontail spotted, stalked, and nailed with bow and arrow. "There's just no feeling, no accomplishment, quite like it," one long-time archer told me. And I believe him.

There are benefits of bowhunting other than the personal ones, too. Most states offer archery hunting seasons well ahead of gun seasons, which means bowhunters are in the woods during early fall when the weather is fine and the game has not yet been scattered by gunfire and red-coated armies of riflemen. Bowhunting licenses and permits are sometimes less expensive than those required of gunmen. Several states in the West hold elk bowhunts in late August and September, smack in the middle of the elk's rutting and bugling season.

Try practicing with your .30-30 or 12-gauge in your backyard and you won't have to poll the neighbors for their opinion—they will come to you. But archery is silent and much safer for suburban practice with only minor preparation for keeping your arrows out of the neighborhood dogs. One chap I know lives near the downtown section of his city, but a few bales of straw, a canvas tarp, and a little paint provide him with a safe, effective backstop for the dozens of arrows he shoots in weekly practice. In fact, his sessions have been known to draw neighbors to his backyard, so intrigued are they by a grown man playing with bows and arrows. They snicker at his archery tackle but welcome venison steaks without a second thought.

Arrows

Any discussion of archery tackle might logically begin with the bow, but I prefer to begin with arrows because of the simple fact that arrows are the core of good, or bad, shooting. You can shoot quality arrows reasonably well from a poor bow, but no one yet has been able to do well shooting poor arrows from even the most expensive bow.

An arrow is said to have spine; that is, its rigidity is matched to the draw weight of the bow. Most commercially produced arrows offer a bit of tolerance, meaning you are likely to buy arrows spined for 45 to 50 pounds for a 45-pound bow. Spine is very important because of the physics involved. When an arrow is released from a bow, it literally bends around the handle of the bow on departure. How quickly it straightens into on-line flight depends on the power of the bow's thrust and the spine (stiffness) of the arrow.

Today most arrows are made of one of three basic components—wood, aluminum, or fiberglass. Wood is usually less expensive to use (and lose), although archers who insist on the best often go to aluminum or fiberglass. Aluminum arrows are tubular, quite strong, and can withstand a lot of use without cracking or bending. Modern machining methods have developed aluminum and fiberglass arrows that permit less tolerances, fly truer, and last longer.

The feathers on an arrow, sometimes called fletching, catch the air passing along the shaft and force the arrow's tip out front. They are usually made of goose or turkey feathers because these quills contain stiff fibers that hold up well. Most arrows carry three feathers, although I have seen shafts with as many as five separate feathers. Special fiber-

Flu-flu arrows, which this hunter has used to bag his pheasant, carry large, air-grabbing feathers that halt the arrow's flight at a range of about 30 yards.

glass arrows, used for bowfishing and carrying a barbed tip, have fletching of plastic or soft rubber, the better to withstand water.

On the standard arrow containing three feathers, two are of a single dull color or have no special coloration at all, and are known as hen feathers. One feather, usually in a contrasting color, is known as the cock feather and is positioned perpendicular to the bowstring when the arrow is in shooting position. Perpendicular to the cock feather is the nock of the arrow, that bright plastic tip bearing a deep slot in which the bowstring sits when the arrow is drawn. The nock is usually brightly colored in white or yellow so that, even on a camouflaged arrow, lost shafts may be more easily found if they miss the mark and go zinging off into heavy cover.

Feathers on all quality arrows have a slight corkscrew-type twist that serves to put a spin on the arrow in flight, and thereby stabilizes it. This is especially true on heavy hunting arrows where the size of the feathers may also be increased. Most arrows spin in a clockwise direction.

The flu-flu arrow, used for bowhunting birds, squirrels, and other creatures requiring a skyward shot, looks odd but does its job nicely. Feathers on the flu-flu, instead of lying back parallel to the shaft, are fletched perpendicular to the arrow so they stand straight up. When shot for an upward-positioned angle, the flu-flu's odd feathers permit normal arrow flight for a distance of about 30 yards, then straighten, grab the air, and drop the shaft straight down to earth—unless, of course, you hit that flushing ringneck or squirrel. But missed shots with flu-flu arrows mean the hunter can recover his arrow, and this is the important thing.

I remember a pheasant hunt when my arrow neither missed nor came down. One of our hunters spotted a fat pheasant sitting on a tree branch some 40 feet off the ground and decided to make sure he went home with meat by potting it off the limb. He drew his bow and I got ready to back him up. His shot narrowly missed the bird but rattled against the tree and flushed the bird to flight. I released my arrow and it plunked the bird squarely in the chest, penetrating a good 5 inches behind its broadhead point. All this seemed lost on the bird, however, because it flew off cackling, my arrow dangling ridiculously behind. If it hadn't been for my Brittany spaniel, the bird would have been lost, along with my arrow.

Arrowheads

There are nearly as many types of arrowheads on the market today as there are hunters to use them. Some are designed for practice, some for small game, and some for the continent's biggest game. Fortunately, modern arrows are of uniform model types and diameters, and heads of several types can be screwed onto arrows interchangeably. All that's necessary is that each head be of identical weight in grams.

It's a good idea to inspect all broad-heads during the hunting day, especially those that have been shot. Dirt, leaf bits, and other debris can make arrows shoot poorly.

Of the five general types of arrow points, the target point should be of interest to the beginner bowman. These small, rounded, metal points are designed to penetrate most backstops. They are light and fly well and are seen in many Olympic competitions and tryouts. Everything about these competition arrows spells speed, including their trim target heads. Shot from amazingly complex bows by talented target archers, these shafts attain incredible accuracy.

The field point is longer and has the shape of a pointed bullet. They are used for field plunking and some small-game hunting. Big-game hunters have been known to carry one along with big-game broadheads, just in case a grouse or hare is spotted within range. But, alas, more than one elk or deer hunter has, in the excitement of the moment, bounced a field arrow harmlessly off the ribs of some big game, sending it into the next county.

The blunt tip, sometimes called a bludgeon, relies on shocking power and is used on small game such as birds, rabbits, and squirrels. Blunt-tipped arrows are fully capable of breaking wings or killing instantly with headshots, although a solid hit in the body has been known to fail to drop the game immediately. I have seen cock ringnecks hit smack in the body with bludgeon-tipped arrows go right on flying, although certainly severely bruised. Those archers who like to hunt sitting rabbits find the blunt effective, since most sitting rabbits are taken in the head.

Another type of hunting head for arrows which is used mainly on small, fast game like squirrels, is known as the grabber or judo head. It includes four short, stiff wires attached perpendicular to the head itself. These, along with the head, are driven into the game on impact and help anchor the arrow while doing internal damage.

The broadhead hunting arrow, in one form or another, has been in use since man first lashed a flake of flint to a small spear and called it an arrow. In fact, the only uniformity among the lot is in the name—the contraption is broad and does form the head, or front, of the arrow. From that point things get complex.

Hunting broadheads come with two, three, four, or even five cutting edges. Some heads are smooth and scalpel-sharp, some carry built-in barbs, and at least one is shaped like an apple corer, supposedly to bore its own little hole upon impact. One popular broadhead has two permanent steel edges, plus a pair of tiny slots where dart-shaped razor blades are inserted for additional cutting. And several heads are available that feature rounded points and four razor inserts that may be sharpened or replaced as needed.

Whatever the type, the broadhead is supposed to be sharp enough to slice its way through hide, muscle, cartilage, and even small bones, on the way to heart, lungs, liver, and large arteries. Unlike the bullet, which kills by shock, the hunting head must, in the case of big game, kill the animal by bleeding it to death internally. A broadhead that isn't extremely sharp is worse than no arrow at all. It does not penetrate well, does a poor job of cutting at best, and often results in game running off and suffering—and probably dying—needlessly. As a bowhunting compadre of mine put it: "The man who hunts with dull arrows should have his bow broken in two and be banned from the woods."

An owner of prime Midwestern whitetail country tells me he permits no bowhunters on his land because of what he has seen with his own eyes.

"It used to be every fall I'd see four or five deer running around with arrows sticking out of their bodies. I finally got sick of it and stopped letting archers hunt here," he said. Whatever the reason those deer weren't killed cleanly, it can be traced to the hunter who used inferior equipment or perhaps took an inadvisable shot.

On the positive side, the fact that a hunter uses a bow rather than firearms can work in his favor. A farmer I know refuses hunting permission to gunners seeking deer, saying he dislikes hearing the occasional gunfire. Yet it only took one year of having too many deer on his place—gobbling his soybeans and corn, mashing flat a ten-acre wheat field—before he welcomed bowhunters with open arms. He believed the light hunting pressure by archers would move some of the deer elsewhere and permit his crops to reach harvest, and he was right.

Bows

There are three types of bows on the market today (excluding cross-bows, which are legal for hunting in relatively few states). The first is the longbow, a style that goes back more than a thousand years. The weapon is well named. It is rather long, sometimes reaching a strung length of 6 feet, which makes it unhandy in dense cover or a small tree-stand. The longbow is known for the smoothness of its draw and release and today is usually constructed of solid wood or fiberglass. This is an excellent bow with which to break into archery because of its simplicity and ease of use.

Of probably even more ancient vintage is the recurve bow, used many centuries ago by Near Eastern civilizations for hunting and in war. The recurve bow is beautiful in its efficiency and simplicity. Its design permits the bow to be quite short in overall length while losing no power. It can easily be used from horseback or in heavy cover and develops more raw thrust with the same amount of draw than does its longbow cousin.

The most recently developed bow is the compound, which looks like something out of a physics exam for practical jokers. The compound is permanently strung and can be adjusted for whatever draw weight the archer prefers. Drawing the bow requires much less muscle power, and the bow becomes easier to pull the farther the bow is drawn. This is of value to the deer hunter, for example, because he can spot his buck approaching, draw his bow, and hold in the full-draw position until he has a clear shot.

Sometimes newcomers to the compound underestimate its power, as I did one October afternoon while deer hunting on some Army property in Kentucky. A nice little eight-point buck ambled by about 50 yards from my tree stand, even pausing broadside while I drew a brand-new compound bow. At that range, I estimated that the arrow would drop about 8 inches and so held that far above the buck's lung area. I released and watched the arrow close on the deer, only to skim the animal's back 8 inches high! The arrow's trajectory had been dead-on at about 50 yards, and had I known that, the deer would have been mine. As it was, the arrow rattled off through the woods—and so did the deer.

Practice, practice, practice. This is the dictum preached by those who would make sure that neophytes start off right in bowhunting. It is a difficult instruction to fault, considering that consistent success with this most ancient of weaponry depends on doing everything right every time. Certainly total familiarity of the archer with his tackle is to be recommended highly.

Accessories

Bowhunters, like trapshooters and golfers, have a long list of accessories designed to do small but necessary jobs. Foremost, of course, is something in which to carry arrows. A quiver of any type should do several things well. It should carry at least four extra arrows in such a position that they can be reached quickly and in the right position. It should also provide some sort of covering over the fragile (and dangerous) hunting heads. A good quiver must carry several arrows without crushing the feathers on any of them, and without permitting the shafts to rattle together as the hunter walks.

There are several types of quivers on today's market that do all of these things. Most popular is the bow quiver that attaches, temporarily or permanently, to the bow itself and holds up to eight arrows. Each shaft is anchored between hard rubber clips that separate each arrow from the others. The bow quiver is attached on the side of the bow opposite the side used by the archer for sighting and releasing. It keeps the arrows handy and usually includes a hard-surface hood that mantles the heads and protects them.

The belt and pocket quivers usually hold fewer shafts than the bow quiver (these quivers seldom hold more than five arrows). The belt model clamps to the hunter's belt over the hip on his draw-hand side, while the pocket model is slipped into a rear pocket on the same draw side.

The back quiver hangs down over the archer's back by means of a strap over the shoulder and another across the chest to keep the quiver from slipping out of position. This type of quiver can accommodate a dozen or more arrows but has the disadvantages of allowing the arrows to rub against one another, rattle, and make noise when an arrow is drawn from the quiver. Modern back quivers often contain one or more zippered pockets for small items, plus a built-in knife sheath and some leather thongs for odd chores afield.

Here's a tip: If arrows in your back quiver rattle too much, pluck a handful of light weeds, roll them into a ball, and shove this ball into the bottom of your quiver. Then replace the arrows. Now held somewhat apart by the weeds, the arrows should no longer rattle and rub together. Few big-game bowhunters opt for back quivers today.

Another tackle accessory that few dedicated archery hunters are without is some type of shooting glove. The glove covers the tips of the fingers used to draw the bow, protecting them from the finger pinch characteristic of shorter bows and from the considerable abrasion of

The serious bowhunter must have at least a minimum of accessories. This archer uses a leather shooting glove and one of several styles of bowstring silencers.

repeated drawing and releasing of a powerful bow. Most gloves come fitted for three-finger use.

The finger tab is a less involved and cheaper way to protect fingertips. It is merely an oval-shaped patch of soft leather with a small hole that fits over the shooting hand's middle finger, which holds it in place. The tab does little to protect fingers from string pinch, however.

It is very important that the arrow is placed on the bowstring at exactly the same point every time a shot is made because this controls the elevation of the arrow in flight. The moment your game clears the trees is no time to fumble with correct nocking when you should already be at full draw and sighting. Most bowhunters use soft rubber or metal nocking points permanently attached to the bowstring. The rubber models are usually bean-shaped and have a hole through the middle. The pair of nocking points is slipped over the end of the bowstring and slid into place at the correct point on the string.

A second type of nocking point is a strip of metal wrapped around the string at the correct point, then crimped into place. Arrow nocks rest atop this contrivance.

Some hunters also use a wrist guard, a piece of metal-ribbed leather that is lashed to the wrist of the bow hand. The string of the released bow slaps the guard, not the wrist itself. Some hunters prefer to do without the guard, especially those whose shooting style seldom includes wrist slap by the bowstring.

Nearly all game animals react to the strum or twang of a released bowstring. Some even manage to get out of the way of an arrow already on its way. The string silencer is the answer. It comes in several shapes and materials, and acts as a tiny shock absorber that deadens the sound of the string. In most cases two silencers are used per bow, one on each end of the string. They are made of soft rubber, fiber, or leather. A simple piece of yarn about 4 inches long, tied to the string near each limb of the bow, has the same effect.

Recurve bows used in dense cover have a way of attracting twigs and weeds that become lodged between the string and the bow limb. I like to use small rubber brush buttons, about the diameter of a quarter, which slide onto the string and are positioned so that they just touch the limb of the bow at rest. Buttons add no appreciable weight to the bow and keep trash from fouling between string and limbs.

Perhaps the most important accessory used by bowhunters is something to sharpen broadheads. Heads scraped against weeds and brush can quickly lose that fine cutting edge, and sometimes need touching up. I like to carry a small sharpening stone in the pocket of my back quiver, or in a shirt pocket if a bow quiver is used. It gives me something to do between shots, too.

Proper clothing for the bowhunter should be warm, roomy enough to give when the bow is drawn, and of a dark color that will blend into cover when hunting big game. It should be of a soft fiber that will be relatively quiet when scraped against brush.

You'll probably need a stout rope at least 20 feet long if you hunt big game. It's much safer to tie the rope to your bow before climbing into a tree stand, then drawing the bow up after you. And, of course, you'll want something to serve as a drag when you haul that big whitetail out of the woods.

Tips on Hunting

For any bowhunter, it is important to know your quarry well enough to be able to locate it and get close to it. Long, arching bowshots may be picturesque, but they often result in lost arrows or, worse yet, wounded game that is never found. Get close enough so that you really can't miss. You owe it to the game, to the sport, and to yourself as a hunter who has taken up the most difficult, and for some the most satisfying, way of matching yourself against the game and the woods.

Poor shots are at least as easy to make with archery gear as with firearms, maybe more so. Even well-placed hunting arrows seldom drop the animal in its tracks, and you can imagine the effects of a poor hit on almost any animal. For most of us, the bow is a limited-range weapon. I hesitate to shoot much beyond 40 yards, and will always delay if chances are good of getting even closer to the game. This not only cuts the margin of error but is just as sporting as long-distance shooting, because there is nothing easy about pussyfooting up on a wary old buck

There he goes! Wingshooting with a bow means getting that shot off fast.

or watching one amble closer to a tree stand while your heart tries to beat a hole in your chest.

I've used bow camouflage for years and believe it to be invaluable in helping me blend into the foliage. Bow camouflage comes in two forms, elastic tape and the full bow sock. In my opinion, tape is the better of the two because it matches exactly the contours of the bow and does a good job of shutting off reflection. The bow sock is a cloth affair of camouflage material that fits over the bow's limbs. I've found socks to be rather bulky and noisy in the woods and suspect they may slow the bow speed a bit.

Where to aim on small and big game with a bow and arrow? About the same places you would if hunting with a rifle. The game's vital spots don't change just because you are using archery gear. On big game offering a broadside shot, by all means put your shaft into the area just behind and slightly below the shoulder. Here are located the lower edge of the lungs, the liver, and the heart. Of the three organs, the lungs are probably the easiest and most desirable target. They are about the size of a pie plate on the average deer or elk and are blood-gorged. A solid

Many archers use the corner of the mouth as a comfortable point at full draw. The three-finger grasp on the bowstring is also comfortable and permits a smooth release.

hit here with a scalpel-sharp broadhead will quickly put the animal down from loss of blood, although it may run several hundred yards. This run is all to the good, however; the animal is merely speeding the inevitable.

Sometimes bowhunters make poor shots but get lucky. A friend was hunting deer in Kentucky when a dandy eight-pointer ambled under his stand. The hunter slightly miscalculated the downward angle of the shot and put his shaft directly between the buck's shoulders from overhead. It died immediately, its spine nearly cut in two. In fact the arrow penetrated less than 4 inches.

On small game, the headshot is the surest, and one of the toughest. A cottontail's head is about 3½ inches long, and a sitting cottontail draws that head downward while squatting among the weeds, so the archer has perhaps 3 square inches at which to shoot. Add to this the problem of shooting at a nearby animal at a downward angle and you realize why some impossible-to-miss shots don't put meat in the pan. In fact, if you plan to hunt sitting cottontails much, it pays to walk slowly through the fields and woods before the season opens. Let your eyes flit back and forth and choose a bright leaf or stump, quickly drawing the bow and releasing. You'll be surprised at the number of nearby targets you will miss until the hands catch up with the eye. Practiced enough, however, the close-up target will become almost automatic and you'll hit every bunny you shoot at.

One final tip. There may be better tune-up animals for deer hunting

Many so-called varmints offer off-season shooting opportunities that keep hunting skills keen. This marmot is a favorite bowhunters' target. (Photo courtesy Canadian Government Travel Bureau)

around than the common and lowly groundhog, but if so I don't know of any. The groundhog, also called woodchuck, pasture pig, or whistle pig, is very wary, blessed with excellent eyesight and hearing, and common enough in the eastern United States to provide great bowhunting.

Although groundhogs may dig their main den just inside a woodline or brushy fencerow, this critter does most of its feeding out in the open on corn, soybeans, truck crops, and even garden vegetables. Like a whitetail deer, it is not an easy animal to stalk. It is also a tough little animal and you are by no means committing overkill if you use your deer tackle for groundhogs. This has the obvious advantage of keeping you and your muscles in tune for deer through the summer months, and come fall you can move right to deer with no change in tackle.

In the West, rock chucks and other woodchuck cousins not protected by closed seasons can provide excellent tune-ups for big-game bow-hunting, not to mention providing great sport on their own. And if you can stalk close enough to these plentiful pasture pigs to put a shaft where you want it, I'd say you're ready for deer.

Chapter 9

FIELD CARE

Care of Large Game

The first step in any field dressing chore of a large game animal is to make sure the animal you're about to open is in fact really dead. This avoids getting kicked or run over, not to mention having the boys back at camp make you the laughing stock of the week. Coming up on an animal the hunter thought was dead—but wasn't—isn't funny, and sometimes it can be nearly tragic.

Once you know for sure the game is dead, you are free to go about the messy but necessary business of putting that animal in shape for the table, be it buffalo or grouse, deer or cottontail. In fact, how that meat tastes on the table is entirely in your hands from the moment it drops until it sizzles in the frying pan. Wild game can be wonderful or insufferable on the table, depending in large part on how quickly it is opened, cleaned, and cooled. Provided the air temperature is cool enough to retard spoilage, a properly cleaned animal must be really messed up in the kitchen in order not to taste good.

There are three factors that will combine to ruin your game meat unless you see to it that they have no chance to do so. These are heat, bacteria found in blood, and intestinal juices released when your lead or arrow pierces flesh, muscle, and guts. Field dressing releases body heat quickly, removes intestines and blood on which bacteria feed, and drains any fluids released into the body cavity through the wound and subsequent cutting.

Let's say you've planned long and hard for that annual deer hunt and you've hunted well. The shot went true, the deer dropped within 50 yards, and now you are standing over it admiring the rack, the size, and maybe the fine eating and storytelling the animal will provide. But when the exhilaration is over, the dead animal is still lying there for you to care for. Now what?

Field dressing that deer is easier than the inexperienced hunter might think. Properly done, it shouldn't take you more than ten minutes, fifteen minutes at the most, to do a thorough job and have the deer ready to transport.

Start by rolling the animal over on its back, head pointed uphill if a slope is handy so any guts and fluids will automatically sag toward the animals hindquarters. Place your hand on the middle of the animal's chest; you should locate a fist-size spot of soft flesh where the brisket meets the belly. Grab a bit of skin slightly to the rear of the brisket and pull it up a bit. Insert the point of your knife, cutting edge facing upward, just beneath the hide to begin the long incision from brisket to anus. It's a good idea to use one hand on the knife while the other guides the blade so it cuts only the skin of the deer, never the flesh beneath. This is important to ensure that no innards are severed, which would release intestinal fluid into the body cavity to taint the meat.

Continue this careful cut all the way down the animal's belly to the genitals, stopping just before you reach the penis (or the vagina if the deer is a doe). If done right, the cut you've just made parted the belly skin but did not open the body cavity, which comes later.

Move behind the animal and, with one foot on each side of its hindquarters, begin making a circular cut at least 5 inches deep around the anus, as though you were coring an apple. During this cut, you might use your free hand to pinch off the anus to prevent the leakage of any feces. Once the anus has been freed, keep it pinched off while you pull it slightly out of the body and tie it off with a bit of string, a shoelace, or whatever else is handy. Make a similar cut to free the penis from its anchoring tissue and tie it off the same way. Some hunters cut the penis off completely and toss it away, but this permits urine to spill on the meat.

Now you're ready to gut your deer. From deep in the pelvic area make a cut the length of the belly, again taking care not to pierce any intestines or other organs. Continue the cut all the way to the brisket. This will expose the animal's stomach, intestines, bladder, and other organs for easy removal. Run one hand behind (or under) each organ, using the other hand to sever any connecting tissue. Once the exposed organs are freed, move up to the brisket until you find the deer's diaphragm, a thin membrane separating its belly cavity from its chest cavity. This membrane should be trimmed away all the way around the cavity, exposing the lungs and windpipe. Cut any tissue anchoring the lungs to the cavity wall and, reaching as far up inside the chest and neck as you can with one hand, grasp the windpipe and pull it down hard. Then, while still holding the windpipe down with one hand, reach up inside with your knife hand and sever the tube as far up inside the neck as you can reach. After the windpipe is cut free at its upper extremity, it's a simple matter to pull it down into the belly cavity, followed closely by the lungs to which it is attached.

When all the animal's removable guts have been cut free, grab two of the deer's legs on one side and roll it over onto its belly, dumping the guts onto the ground in the process. Many deer hunters carry a roomy, reinforced plastic bag into which goes the animal's heart and liver. The bag can be conveniently placed back inside the deer's body for easy transport if the deer is to be dragged any distance.

Placing the deer on its belly, especially if it is facing uphill, hurries the drainage of blood and fluids and debunks the notion that you must pig-stick a deer in the throat in order to bleed it sufficiently. Gutting the animal removes all necessary blood, if you follow up by draining the carcass well and wiping the body cavity nearly dry afterwards. Wait a few minutes so all excess moisture has drained away, then roll the animal onto its back again and do a good job of wiping the cavity clean. Use a towel if you have it, although a handful or two of dry leaves, balled weeds, or dry pine needles will suffice in a pinch. Scrub the rib cage until it shines; this removes bacteria-breeding moisture and retards spoilage.

Elk, moose, and caribou are field dressed in virtually the same manner as deer; the anatomy is similar and the only real difference is the size of the carcass. If the animal happens to die lying on its back, one man can probably do the job of gutting out his kill. But if that elk or moose must be rolled over before dressing can begin, you'll need either a willing companion or a winch.

There's also the problem of getting the meat from the spot where it dropped back to camp, your car, or the nearest road. Deer, even big whitetails and muleys, are not much of a problem in relatively flat country. They are simply dragged headfirst with the front feet tied securely behind the head. But for a deer to be moved out of deep canyons and arroyos is another ball game indeed. You'll have to do a lot of grunting and groaning to move that dead weight up much of a slope, and you may have to use a packhorse or even rig a long rope from the deer to the rear axle of a motor vehicle.

North America's largest antlered game—elk, moose, and caribou—are nearly always cut into quarters before being moved. This makes transporting the meat much easier, plus helps speed the carcass's cooling process.

I was in a party of elk hunters when one of the hunters dropped an animal 5 miles of trail and 3,000 feet of altitude above camp. Three men spent an hour dressing the animal, and another hour removing its hide and cutting it into quarters for transport down the mountain. This is where the outfitter's string of horses came in handy. Each horse was

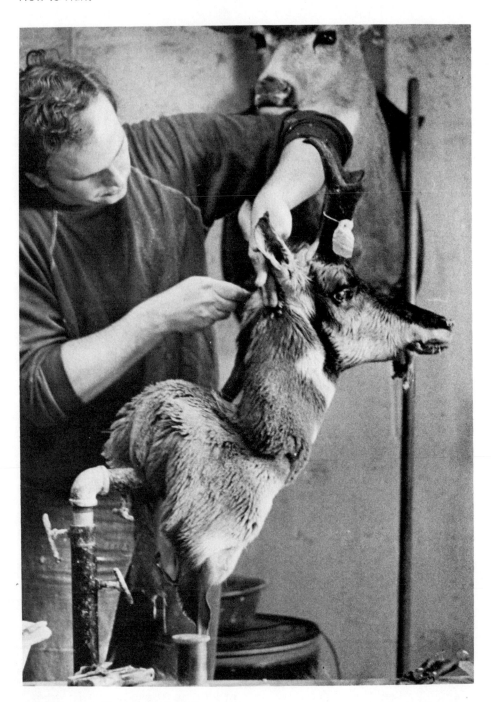

A taxidermist fits an antelope cape on a pre-cast form. Careful field care of trophy heads and capes assures a handsome mount later on.

carrying a pack saddle; the first horse carried a balanced load of two elk quarters, one on each side of the saddle and lashed to prevent movement. Another horse carried the remaining two quarters, and a third toted the hide, head, and antlers. So well-conditioned were those horses that a startled coyote running from trailside brush failed to halt their progress down the mountain. I would have thought the smell of all that blood and guts might have caused a bit of eye-rolling and nervous prancing, but these veteran animals merely stood quietly while being loaded with no more restriction than ground-tied lead ropes.

Once the animal has been moved to the location where it is to be hung and hided, be it camp or home, the entire carcass should be hung up headfirst. Hang it high enough so the hind feet clear the ground. If your game is a trophy with head and horns worthy of a den wall, you'll want to cape out the front shoulders, neck and head for special care and delivery to the taxidermist.

Caping a game head isn't difficult and requires only a sharp, 5-inch knife and perhaps a small saw or hatchet. Start by cutting into the hide to the rear of and parallel to the shoulders; continue this cut all the way around the animal's brisket, or even as far back as the rear edge of the brisket. Now, starting where the cut between the shoulders centers on the base of the neck, make a similar hide-deep cut from the withers right up the nape of the animal's neck to the base of its skull. These are the only cuts you'll need for now.

Starting where the neck cut meets that circling the rear shoulders, begin peeling the hide away, rolling it toward the head as you progress. When the hide has been peeled all the way to the head, carefully fold it temporarily out of the way to avoid nicking it, and use a saw or hatchet to sever the head from the upper neck. If this is properly done, you will have provided the taxidermist with all he needs to create a handsome wall mount. Don't worry about the cut along the back of the trophy's neck; this can be sewn together over the mold, and will not be visible on a normal wall mount, anyway.

If the animal is to be cut up for meat right away, run a gambrel (heavy stick with both ends sharpened) through each rear hock and raise the carcass off the ground with a rope tied to the middle of the gambrel. The hiding process begins just above the hocks and continues along both flanks, the back, and finally the neck. Be sure to see that no hair touches the exposed flesh; this can taint the meat and some commercial meat processors feel so strongly about it that meat delivered with any hair stuck to it is immediately trimmed away, followed by a lecture on proper field care.

This brings up another point. Should your animal be commercially butchered, or should you save a few dollars and do the job yourself? I have always chosen the former because when it comes to butchering meat I want the meat to be cut to my order—steaks so thick, so many steaks to the package, etc.—and I want some pork fat mixed with the ground venison. The processor charges me only $20 for the entire job, including the pork addings, and has cold meat lockers available for rent right on the premises if I need them. Special processing, such as having the entire animal ground into deerburger (a waste of great eating), costs somewhat more.

If the game hide is to be saved and used (they make handsome additions to a den wall, or saved up, fine lounging jackets or gloves) you'll have to spend a few minutes fatting and salting the hide. Lay the hide hair-side-down on the ground and gently scrape away as much of the tallow as possible, being careful not to slice into the skin itself. Then use several handsful of salt and rub this into the hide, including the rough edges of the skin where hide meets hair. When the hide is thoroughly salted, roll it up skin-side-in and tuck in the ends of the roll to prevent leakage and store it off the ground in a shady spot for a day or two. Then unroll it, shake the salt off, drain the fluids drawn out by the salt, and resalt it. Roll the hide up and deliver it to your taxidermist. Be sure to specify whether you want the hide tanned with the hair on or off.

Although deer hides with the hair on look rustic when spread across the back of couches and chairs, they aren't practical for this purpose because deer hair is hollow and brittle and easily broken. Sit on such a hide for long and you'll come away with clothes covered with these hairs.

Care of Small Game

For some reason, hunters don't seem to be as aware that small game needs attention afield just as much as large game. Perhaps this is because such critters as cottontails, waterfowl, and upland birds are small enough to be plopped into a game bag or sack until the day is over so the hunt can continue uninterrupted. But place two or three still-warm birds or rabbits into a well-insulated game pocket, keep them there for several hours, and there is no way they will fare as well on the table as birds or rabbits opened, gutted, and cooled immediately after killing.

Steve Roth, a hunting companion of mine and the product of a long line of hunters, showed me a method of field-gutting a freshly killed cottontail that requires no cutting at all and in fact can be accomplished in a minute while you're still pacing along behind the hounds.

Let's assume you've just rolled a rabbit and pick it up. The carcass is still warm and limp. Grasp it with the right hand and give it a shake tail-first to settle the viscera toward the animal's hindquarters. Then slide your left hand down across the animal's shoulders to the rear edge of the rib cage; here you should feel the swelling caused by the viscera inside the body cavity. Tighten your fingers and thumb across the back and push down on the swelling; you should feel it slip a bit as the pressure increases. Still gripping the rabbit with your left hand, move your right hand immediately below your left and take a hard, downward squeeze against the ball of viscera, forcing it toward the rabbit's anus. Done right, this forces the animal's guts—everything to the rear of its diaphragm—down and out the anus. It is then a simple matter to shake or pull the intestines free from the carcass and dispose of them out of the reach of the dogs. I don't recommend this method unless the temperature is well below 40 degrees, however, because it does permit body heat to remain inside the carcass.

For those who prefer to slit open the rabbit's belly, it's a good idea to carry a heavy plastic bag. Gutted and bled rabbits are dropped in the bag that is carried in the game pocket; this keeps blood from soiling your hunting coat or vest.

The skinning of a rabbit is easy if care is taken not to tear its rather thin hide. Start by making a cut around each hind leg just above the first joint; then make a connecting cut down the inside of each thigh. Hold the rabbit head-down and gently pull the skin away from each hind leg; the hide should then peel down the back and belly in a single piece. Trim the hide away from each front leg and continue pulling it free until you reach the base of the skull. Cut off the head and the freed hide along with it, remove the lower portions of all four legs, and trim out the anal area housing the rectum and genitals. The carcass is then washed in cold water and rinsed. Storing the carcass overnight in cold water containing a bit of table salt will draw blood out of punctures made by shot or arrows. If the animal is not to be eaten immediately, the carcass should be cut into serving pieces and frozen.

Upland bird hunters have the choice of plucking or skinning their birds when cleaning time comes, but all birds should be drawn as soon after killing as possible. Some hunters make a small enlargement of the bird's anus, inserting a stick and twisting it to grasp the viscera. The stick is then withdrawn with the guts clinging to it. Others prefer to open the bird's body just below the breast and draw the viscera out by hand. The latter method is probably better because it permits more of the body heat to escape.

If the bird is to be plucked, thereby saving its skin to help contain body juices during cooking, there's no need to incur your wife's wrath by spreading feathers all over the kitchen. Just heat a gallon or so of water to scalding temperature and dip each bird headfirst into the water for about twenty seconds. This reduces the bird's natural body oil (especially true with waterfowl), and makes the wet feathers cling together, which reduces the mess. Grasp some feathers between your fingers and pull them out, starting along the midline of the back and moving to the belly. Remove the leg feathers below the first joint and trim off the legs; do the same to the head and neck.

If you have occasion to hunt quail and doves and don't want to spend the little extra time to pluck your birds, skinning is the answer. This method is especially adaptable to dove and quail because the majority of the edible meat is located in the bird's breast. If the breast meat is all you plan to save, just split the skin in the center of the breast, pull it to each side to expose the swelling of meat underneath, and, reaching in under the breastbone with two fingers, pull the entire breast up toward the chin. I use a pair of meat snips to clip the bit of flesh holding the upper breast to the back of the bird, and can clean half-a-dozen bobwhites in just a few minutes in this way. All that's lost is the morsel of flesh along the upper portions of each leg, and perhaps an even smaller bit at the base of each wing.

And when you're cleaning gamebirds (pheasant and grouse in particular), by all means have a paper sack handy to hold the breast, wing, and tail feathers. Gamebird feathers are so colored as to be in special demand by fly tyers. Even if you don't tie your own flies, you can probably swap the feathers for a couple dozen flies of your own choice. You get the flies virtually free and the fly tyer gets a new supply of rare gamebird hackles. I do this every fall when I've built a supply of grouse wings and tailfans, and I haven't paid for a fly in years. If you don't personally know anyone who ties flies, find out who supplies a local tackle shop and make him an offer.

The amount of large and small game that ends up in the garbage can each fall is astounding. Even more appalling is the fact that so much meat is wasted because the hunter tried and failed to do a proper job of dressing, or, worse yet, was too lazy to undertake the task once the hot blood of the kill had passed. People who would do that make me so angry I'd like to grab one of their ankles in each hand and make a wish. I think an integral part of this business of hunting is keeping a respect for the animal, no matter its size or bragging potential. If you're going to end the life of an elk or a quail, or whatever, respect the animal enough to make full use of what it has to give: sport *and* food. Do less and you as a hunter become the endangered species.

I recall driving home after a week's deer hunt. I'd failed to get my deer and was longingly staring at all the cars on the road bearing handsome whitetail bucks on their rear bumpers and cartop racks. A station wagon carrying two hunters and a pair of fine antlered bucks passed me and I mentally congratulated them on their success. Then I saw something else that almost made me glad I hadn't gotten a deer.

A passenger car went by occupied by two hunters. Across the roof was lashed a big deer that obviously hadn't been properly dressed and drained before its owners headed home. Body fluids mixed with dried blood had bathed the entire car roof, running down to dry on both fenders and even staining the rear window. No one seeing that bloody load would envy the hunter his success, nor could the hunter look forward to good venison if in fact he bothered to butcher the animal. More than likely he took another look at his handiwork on arriving home and, after bragging his kill to friends, dumped it on some country road to smell up the air and make some farmer even more determined to keep hunters off his land. This shouldn't sound far-fetched. It happens every year.

A writer friend of mine insists he will hunt nothing that cannot later be eaten. I've always thought this a bit extreme—it excludes varmint hunting, for one thing—but that was before I hunted with the husband of a friend of my wife. He'd never hunted before and said he'd like to try, so we drove to a nearby woodlot choking with thornbushes and kicked up some cottontails. As luck had it, the chap flushed a cottontail and fired just as the rabbit dived into a thick tangle of thorny bayberries. He seemed reluctant to do battle with the thorns so I volunteered to retrieve his rabbit. I lay flat on the frozen ground and, by wiggling a bit and reaching a lot, managed to pull his rabbit out of the thorns. I got to my feet and held out the rabbit for him to take.

"Oh, I don't want it," he said matter-of-factly. "I don't think we'd like the taste of rabbit. If you don't want it, just throw it away." I was angry enough just then to make one good punch in the nose worth a dozen lesser evils, but I held my tongue and ended the hunt right then. He'd shot the game, it was his to attend to and either consume at table or present to those who would eat it. Instead he was ready to discard a fine meal and go looking for another rabbit to waste.

People like that make me want to throw up.

This can work the other way around, too, when a hunter kills an animal that cannot be eaten, and does it just for the apparent hell of it.

I was hunting with a forest ranger and his twelve-year-old son one fall. We walked past some wild bushes and the man pointed to a small songbird in a bush and told his son to shoot the bird. Some time later the boy did so, retrieving the small gray-feathered carcass long enough to have a quick look before chucking it into some trailside weeds. If many twelve-year-olds are raised to disrespect protected wildlife like this, heaven help the law-abiding hunters of tomorrow searching for a place to hunt. Cleaning and consuming the game we kill is often the only thing keeping the antihunters off our necks. Do away with this and we are naked to our enemies.

On the other hand, it is entirely possible for just one meal of well-cleaned and prepared game meat to begin changing the mind of a devoted antihunter. I once worked as outdoor columnist for a large city newspaper. I was subjected to a good deal of kidding during hunting season, and the main antagonist was our department's executive sports editor. Every time I went off to hunt deer he accused me of shooting Bambi, and that sort of thing.

So one year I offered him a frozen package of venison chops and gave him a couple of cooking tips to go with them. He took them home with the promise he'd put them on a charcoal grill that very evening. The following day all he could do was rave about how great the chops tasted under a basting of barbeque sauce. This chap by no means turned into a deer hunter as the result of one meal—he'll probably continue to razz all hunters—but at least he knows that properly prepared game meat can be as good or better than the best steak he buys at the butcher shop. I didn't make a new friend for hunters, but perhaps I eliminated one unnecessary enemy.

Chapter 10

START THEM RIGHT

"Daddy, can I go hunting with you?"

Once these words are spoken by your young son or daughter, two special things happen. First, you acquire what will probably become a dependable and lifelong hunting buddy. Second, the job (if that's the right word) of teaching that youngster the safe way to hunt falls to you as the logical instructor to whom he'll look up with those bright eager eyes.

This is pretty heavy stuff, considering that the pupil will carry your instructions for the rest of his active life. What's more, since they come from you, he'll be certain they are all correct and beyond questioning. So it behooves you to do it right.

I've decided that teaching a youngster to hunt is similar to being a parent for the first time: The prospect of having another person look to you for proper guidance can be a scary prospect indeed, so you use what common sense you have to guide him along, and hope it's enough. Thank heavens, it usually is.

Most kids develop a desire early to go afield for the first time. Their desire is ahead of their budding good judgment and they can be downright unsafe with a firearm in their hands, so it's usually best to take them along for a season or two as a sort of unarmed junior partner. This gives you the chance to breathe easy when your back is turned, and to point out the right way to cross a wire fence or track a rabbit while you have the youngster's undivided attention. Make it clear that you expect the lad to retain your lessons before giving him a firearm of his own and he'll likely make an effort to learn if only to shorten the wait.

Sometimes the teaching is better left to someone other than fathers. This is especially true if a relative or close friend is more experienced

Firearms have a natural attraction for young boys; this is the time to encourage safe gun handling and respect for guns.

than you. My father never hunted—it was something that just never interested him—so the responsibility sort of evolved to a great uncle, who had retired and had the time and inclination to take a greenhorn under his wing.

Uncle Frank had hunted for more than sixty years when I came along, all eager-eyed and anxious. He'd taught three boys of his own to hunt, had owned pointers and setters for years, and seemed to enjoy having me with him. A strict disciplinarian afield, he chastised me harshly when I carelessly let a shotgun barrel point his way, left a farmer's gate open, or failed to unload my shotgun before crossing a fence. I was young, and the lessons stuck.

My uncle knew better than to wade into a weed field and hope to jump a rabbit or a covey of bobwhites. He knew that game preferred the edges of fields adjacent to dense fencerows or woodlots, and this is where we looked for game. If we'd been blessed with an inch or two of fresh snow, he'd point out sets of tracks and then quiz me about them. What animal made the tracks? Which way was it going? Was the animal walking or running? How old were the tracks, and so on. After a season or two I could read sign about as well as my tutor and I was pleased that the ability almost always meant seeing more game.

"This snow has been on the ground for a week, and it's crusted hard," Frank would comment with a sly smile. "The rabbits can't get at the grass under the crust, so where should we look for them?"

The answer, I learned, was in woods where the cottontails could eat the bark off saplings above the snow. He also showed me a trick to jump tight-sitting rabbits out of heavy ground cover, such as blackberry thickets or honeysuckle patches. "Rabbits have tight nerves and they'll flush if they think you've discovered them," Frank would say. He'd wade into thigh-deep cover, shuffle his feet a few times and then stand still, his shotgun raised and ready. Often a rabbit would decide he'd been spotted and he'd scoot away from underfoot, but my uncle's load of No. 6 shot usually got in the way.

When the time came for me to get my first shotgun, at the age of ten, my uncle had a say-so in my father's eventual choice. At the time I didn't think much of the choice, but I later came to appreciate the forethought that went into making it.

It was an H & R Deluxe Topper single-shot 16-gauge with a rabbit-ear

A youngster's first hunting experience should be a good one. Here, Mark Smith of Missouri is obviously pleased with his first cottontail rabbit.

hammer and a full-choke barrel. It would shoot only once before needing another load and it taught me to be selective with my shots and to take a fine pointing aim. I usually killed what I shot at, or missed it altogether, avoiding cripples.

The old Topper easily separated into three sections and I quickly learned to break it down after each hunt and wipe it clean of weed seeds, dirt, and fingerprints, use solvent and light oil in the bore, and reassemble it before cleaning my game. After ten years of use by a boy who thought no brier thicket was too painful to penetrate, the shotgun needed only a new sear pin to be as good as new, and several years later I sold it for its original purchase price. I wish I'd kept it.

I think the choice of a 16-gauge was a good one, even if the trend today has been to ignore the sixteen while the twelves and twenties have their flings of popularity. The 16-gauge had punch enough for anything I was likely to hunt, including deer, but the blast wasn't quite as loud to my young ears as a 12-gauge would have been. In fact I quickly learned to disregard the sound of the shotgun when a rabbit or a bob flushed. Not that there's anything wrong with a 12- or a 20-gauge, of course. Each has accounted for a great deal of fine sport. But the 20-gauge has a somewhat limited killing punch, even though it is light enough for even a youngster to tote all day. The twelve certainly has the punch and the pattern for about anything the hunter is likely to seek, but its roar and overall weight make it questionable for a first-gun choice.

Whichever shotgun you choose for your youngster, do stay away from the .410 if the lad is going to be shooting at game instead of clay targets or tin cans. I've heard folks say the .410 is the only choice for a lad's first hunting gun because of its light report and lack of recoil, but this neglects the most important requirement: killing game cleanly. Give a boy a .410 and it is all but certain he will cripple rather than kill the first few birds or bunnies he shoots at. Crippling game is the quickest way I know to turn a youngster off from the hunting sports; in fact I've met men in their fifties who recall early days when game was crippled and a potential lifetime of hunting pleasures was eliminated by the memory. Give your son or daughter something that will do the job.

The halcyon days of your youngster's first season afield are an excellent time to reexamine your own hunting habits for flaws. If you're in the habit, conscious or otherwise, of blasting away at songbirds when game is scarce, firing into heavy weeds at a sound rather than at game itself, or other such idiot practices, it is a certainty that any youngster who hunts with you will grow old doing the same things. It's sort of like teaching a sixteen-year-old to drive; he picks up your good habits along with your bad habits and keeps them forever.

I believe that good hunting etiquette (and that's the right word) merely means showing a basic respect for the other guy, and that includes the

The wrong way to cross a wire fence. Lone hunters should pass the shotgun under the fence, then use both hands in crossing. Take care not to damage the fence.

landowner as well as your hunting partner. I doubt you'd appreciate some fellow from another neighborhood mashing your yard shrubs or trampling your flowers or even harassing your wife's cat, and farmers are no different. Farms are private property, and don't you forget it.

Back when I was writing a newspaper column I interviewed half-a-dozen farmers whose lands were posted against hunting. I wanted to know why their places were verboten, and to a man they blamed careless, boorish hunters who chased stock, broke fences, and, worst of all, hunted without permission. Abuse a farmer once too often and he'll post his land, which affects far more people than just the offenders. It means the hunters of today and tomorrow will have less land to hunt in a time when the ranks of hunters are increasing. That means less quality hunting, and could result in the loss of the sport to all but the privileged few.

So, if your field habits are poor and you think that the basic hunting-gun handling instruction should come from another source, all is not lost. Several national and state organizations offer instructional classes and seminars aimed at teaching youth to be safe with firearms.

It's a good bet that the fish and game or conservation department of your own state government offers hunter safety courses each year. These classes, which last an average of eight hours, are held from late summer right through till the opening of hunting seasons. Such courses, usually funded in part by federal matching funds, teach the youngsters how firearms work, how they can be safely handled, and the best ways to transport the guns from home to field and back again. At the end of each course, written examinations are given, and successful students are rewarded with a cloth patch, ID card, or some other token of completion.

Several states require the course for youngsters under a minimum age before hunting licenses can be purchased. And some big-game states, such as Colorado, require nonresident hunters born after a specified year to show proof of course completion before big-game tags and permits can be obtained.

An excellent booklet on such clinics, entitled "Young Hunters Safety Clinic," is offered by the National Shooting Sports Foundation, 1075 Post Road, Riverside, Connecticut 06878. The booklet contains virtually everything you need to know to plan, equip, and conduct a hunting safety clinic, and tells where the necessary kits may be obtained. The whole program has a package price within the working budget of most established sportsmen's clubs, civic groups, and youth programs. I can think of no finer gift for such a group to give the youth of their community. Often a local newspaper can be enlisted in the effort, sharing the cost and offering the required publicity.

The National Rifle Association has long been a supporter of youth instruction in shooting and hunting. There are plans for the NRA to purchase and put together a large institution where youngsters can be taught to handle firearms and hunt safely and develop a healthy respect for the out-of-doors. Large-scale programs such as this, along with the cooperation of major arms and ammunition manufacturers, bode well for the future of hunting.

The Trapshooting Hall of Fame, located on the Home Grounds of the Amateur Trapshooting Association at Vandalia, Ohio, is sponsoring and administering a program of instruction for high school and college teachers from all over the country. The plan is to put the shooting sports into school curriculums in every state, including rifle targeting, clay target shooting, and other competitive shooting sports. The ATA plan was conceived to combat the growing antigun sentiment faced by virtually all shooters nationwide, but a side effect is the instruction of youngsters in safe gun handling. And even if a student goes through four years of school in classes about shooting, only to later choose not to continue in the sport, he or she at least knows guns are only as safe or dangerous as the person handling it, and not the evil creatures some newspaper editorials would have us believe. I've told my young daughters, and will tell my infant son, that it really matters little if, on reaching adulthood, they continue to hunt or not. That choice is theirs alone. But I will insist they have every opportunity to see hunting and gun handling for what they truly are. This, added to a respect for the outdoors, will help them make decisions in the future when their old man isn't around to give guidance. That's about all a concerned parent can do.

The fruits of an effective early training are no more apparent than in two friends of mine. Karl and Steve Maslowski, a father-son team of the first order, enjoy each other's company and find hunting to be a mutually enjoyed pleasure. Hunting with these men, it isn't difficult to see some of the older man in the younger. Both can spot a sitting rabbit under a bushel of fallen limbs, and neither misses much when his beagles bring a running cottontail before the gun. Each believes in field dressing his game immediately to keep the meat fresh, and neither makes a hunting partner nervous by carelessly pointing his muzzle askew or blasting away at fenceposts or clods of dirt. These men share a reverence for the out-of-doors that is in no way diminished by the fact that they kill rabbits or quail or deer. They see hunting as a part of, not an intrusion on, the natural scene; hunting with them is a good time whether game is seen and bagged or not.

While big-game hunting is as fine an experience for a lad as it is for his father, such big-game sport is usually thought of as a graduate course in a learning process that began with much smaller game. Kids don't start hunting for squirrels and rabbits just because it's the thing to do; they do so because rabbits and squirrels are great teachers of the basics. In fact, I'll bet my best twin-bore that more kids have broken in on bushytails than any other five game animals combined.

Squirrels are early risers, and so are squirrel hunters. This teaches a youngster to match his efforts with the habits of the quarry. Squirrels live in den trees and eat nuts and field crops, often near water, and this teaches a young boy or girl just starting out where to look for the game. Squirrels have good eyes and ears, and this teaches the youngster to move quietly through the woods. Squirrels make small noises when they gnaw on shells or scramble across bark, and this teaches the lad to trust his ears and interpret what they tell him. And finally, squirrels are small and can absorb a lot of misplaced lead, and this teaches young hunters to wait for a good shot, and then make it count. You get my drift. Elk and deer are also active early in the day and have habits that the hunter must know about before hunting begins. Many kinds of game make noises in moving and feeding, and *all* game animals deserve the best efforts of a hunter determined to make a quick kill, or not shoot at all. Squirrels, and an adult to spoon-feed the lessons, can teach a lad a lot.

Last November I took my eight-year-old daughter quail hunting for the first time. She carried no shotgun, of course, but had been after me to take her afield all fall, so off we went. My old Brittany cast through a picked cornfield and went on point at the end of a thick fencerow. My daughter and I moved in behind the dog and up went the birds, scattering on the flush like wind-blown leaves. The first barrel missed cleanly but the second folded a cockbird that my dog raced off to retrieve. The rest of the covey settled into the fencerow ahead.

I took the bird from my dog and handed it over to Kelly for close examination. She smiled at the bird's handsome plumage, smoothed its brown and white neck feathers, and turned it over in her hand. "Are you sure it was all right to shoot this bird, Daddy?" she asked. "It's awfully pretty."

The question gave me an opportunity to point out that at least a dozen other birds in the covey had escaped untouched, more than enough to replace any birds that hunters might take during the hunting season. I told her even more birds would starve if the winter was harsh, and perhaps two or three might be caught by foxes or owls. But come spring, enough birds would remain to nest and produce more quail, and this was the reason it was all right to shoot the bird. She seemed to accept that and was just as excited when the spaniel found a single hiding a few yards away in the fencerow.

The nine-year-old son of a hunting and fishing buddy asked to go along on our rabbit hunt one fall. The weather had been wet and mud was everywhere, and by noon the added weight of gumbo on our boots made calling it a day seem like a good idea. The lad had more trouble in the mud than we adults, yet on the way home he said he'd had a ball and wanted to know when we could go again, mud or no mud. The hunting bug had bitten him and the affliction would last a lifetime.

A nephew of mine who lives in Missouri seemed interested in hunting, but his father, no hunter, didn't encourage the interest. During a Christmas visit I whistled up my hounds and the boy and I went rabbit hunting. The hounds cooperated by jumping a fat rabbit and bringing it back right in front of my nephew. He raised the shotgun and waited—and waited—until I was sure he wasn't going to shoot, then rolled the bunny with a neat going-away shot, his first-ever cottontail. When I commented about the long time it took him to shoot, he grinned a little and said he knew the shot he wanted and waited until it presented itself. He was mighty proud of that first rabbit and I was equally proud of his judgment. Maybe some people are just born hunters needing only an opportunity to show their stuff.

There is little doubt that the safe handling of firearms, coupled with sound game-management practices (of which hunting is a part) will go far in seeing that our children and grandchildren have a chance to enjoy sport hunting. For this reason I'm encouraged by two unrelated pieces of legislation that seek to fund instructional programs, one state and one federal.

The state project is in South Dakota where the Game, Fish and Parks Commission has approved a plan submitted by the South Dakota Bowhunters, Inc., to begin a program of bowhunter instruction in the state. The state bowhunter group, which is associated with the National Field Archery Association (NFAA), presented the plan for its parent organization.

The plan calls for improving bowhunter's skills statewide and already some twenty instructors have been certified. The instructors then teach classes set up by NFAA. A spokesman of the state group said courses will teach such skills as safety with archery equipment, bowhunting methods, trailing of game, equipment selection and care. A companion instruction book, entitled *Bowhunting Deer*, has been published by NFAA to serve as a reference manual for the course. Anyone interested in the state group or its plan for instruction can contact its education chairman at 825 S. Euclid, Sioux Falls, South Dakota 57101.

On the federal level, the U.S. House Subcommittee on Fisheries, Wildlife Conservation and the Environment has approved a bill that, if passed, would place an 11 percent excise tax on components of hand-loaded ammunition, with resulting moneys to be added to the Federal Aid in Wildlife Restoration Program. Half the funds would be apportioned to the states for wildlife restoration purposes and half for hunter education and shooting-range construction. The bill was attacked during hearings by a group calling itself the Committee for Humane Legislation, but committee members seemed little impressed by the group's allegations. The bill's chances of passage appear to be good.

Just how significant are young hunters, and what difference does it

Youngsters have a natural curiosity about the outdoors. In some children, this advances into a lifetime of hunting combined with a general enjoyment of the outdoors. (Photo courtesy U.S. Forest Service)

make how they conduct themselves in the field? To answer these important questions, consider a few numbers on the national popularity of hunting nationwide.

In fiscal 1976, a total of over 25 million hunting licenses, tags, permits, and stamps were sold. That's enough individual licenses for one out of every eight Americans—men, women, and children included. If even a small percentage of this number break fences and shoot farm stock when hunting, it can ruin the sport for everyone.

And all those hunters must care about their sport. In 1976 they spent over $163.5 million for the various licenses required, with a percentage of that amount going back into state treasuries for habitat improvement and game management. For the curious among you, Pennsylvania residents led the license parade with 14.8 million sold, followed by Michigan with 8.8 million. Massachusetts was last with barely a million licenses purchased.

Newspaper and television editorials claim sport hunting is passé and today's youth would be better advised to take up macrame and leave such barbaric pastimes alone. Yet take a look at a youngster sneaking up behind a setter on point, or clambering through midnight woods after a pack of coonhounds, and you realize that editorial writers don't really know what they're talking about. We are still human animals. A little above the youth of centuries ago whose brow was smeared with the blood of their first lion, perhaps, but human animals nonetheless. And any society that can spawn 220 million individuals will never find the quietude and peace of a good hunt passé, at least not as long as man can suffer tension and feel a need to get away from the crowds.

We are privileged to pass on the hunting tradition to the young boys and girls who must cope with tomorrow's world. Take him or her by the shoulder and the two of you enjoy a day afield. And good hunting!

INDEX

(boldface numbers refer to illustrations)

L

M

O

P

Q

R

S

T